Saint  *and
Paisianism*

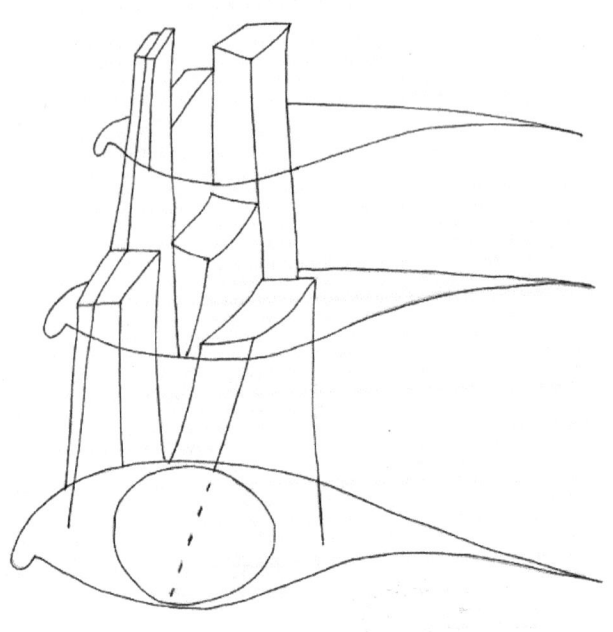

"Look upon me and hear me, O Lord my God. Enlighten my eyes, lest I sleep in death" (*Psalm 12/13:4*).

"Abba Bessarion, at the point of death, said, 'The monk ought to be as the Cherubim and the Seraphim: all eye'" (*The Sayings of the Desert Fathers*, transl. Sister Benedicta, 1975)

Horia Ion Groza

Saint Paisius Velichkovsky of Neamts and Paisianism

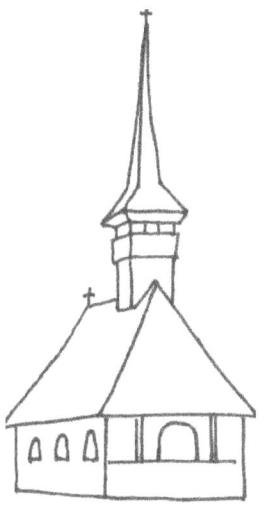

Reflection Publishing

Title: Saint Paisius Velichkovsky of Neamts and Paisianism
Author: Horia Ion Groza
On the cover: Icon of Saint Paisius at St. Herman Monastery, Platina, California, painted by Archpriest Theodore Jurewicz.
Editor: Ioana L. Onica
Line drawings: Horia Ion Groza

The majority of quotations made in this book are from The Orthodox Study Bible, Copyright © 2008 by St. Athanasius Academy of Orthodox Theology.
Old Testament Text:
Scripture taken from St. Athanasius Academy Septuagint™, Copyright © 2008 by St. Athanasius Academy of Orthodox Theology. Used by permission. All rights reserved.
New Testament Text:
Scripture taken from the New King James Version®. Copyright ©1982 by Thomas Nelson, Inc. Used by permission. All rights reserved.

ISBN: 978-1-936629-52-7

COPYRIGHT 2019 © REFLECTION BOOKS

Reflection Publishing, P.O. Box 2182
Citrus Heights, California 95611-2182
E-mail: info@reflectionbooks.com
www.reflectionbooks.com

Contents

Foreword 7
Introduction 15
1. Saint Paisius Velichkovsky of Neamts 29
   1.1. Life of Saint Paisius 29
   1.2. Monastic Contribution of Saint Paisius 67
   1.3. Saint Paisius' Teachings 78
2. Treasure of Paisianism. 86
   2.1. Paisianism in Eastern Europe 87
      2.1.1. Saint Callinicus of Chernika 87
      2.1.2. The Burning Bush Movement 101
      2.1.3. Saint Seraphim of Sarov 116
      2.1.4. The Elders of Optina 126
   2.2. Paisianism in America. 145
      2.2.1. Saint Herman of Alaska 145
      2.2.2. Paisianism in Monastic Life 157
Conclusions 184
Bibliography 216

Foreword

Why should we read about a monk who lived over 200 years ago and worked on the teachings of spiritual Fathers who lived before him, in the period of the fourth to fifteenth centuries?

Before answering this question, we need to consider some general things. We Americans are a people of reasoning. When we fail or reach a lack of progress after methodically building large scaffoldings based on a chain of arguments, proofs and conclusions, we often prefer turning back to square one thinking that our knowledge is missing some chain links. Sometimes even when everything goes satisfactorily, we still feel the need to look back to check if our whole reasoning was on the right track, in order to eliminate all the doubts that persist in bothering us.

The same happens with our philosophy of life and our motivation to live. We go back in memory, we check again, but there are still many things we cannot explain despite all our efforts. However, we cannot wait, we have to go forward, our life is short and we have to find a sense in conjunction with ourselves, society, nature, and the universe. Fortunately, where science is helpless, religion can help; where reason hits a dead-end, faith can go further. "Of course, **God** is not *an object* on which one can do experiments – God inevitabily transcends science," says the English physicist, theologian and Anglican priest John Polkinghorne (Polkinghorne and Beale, 2009). But do we have an *objective* proof about "what constitutes the dark matter and dark energy that seem to make up over 90% of the universe?" If we think further and we admit that a Creator *exists* and, naturally, He is full of love for His creation, we can conclude that He is *personal* and, because as a Master of the Universe He has to cover and control such an immense diversity of aspects of it, He might also be more than personal - He might be a *Trinity*.

"The atoms that make up our bodies are changing all the time, through wear and tear, eating and drinking. What gives continuity are not the atoms themselves but the almost infinitely complex information-bearing pattern in which they are organized," wrote Polkinghorne. "The essence of this pattern is **the soul**." God "will preserve it in the divine memory... Thus, the ultimate Christian hope is resurrection [which is] God's great eschatological act of reimbodiment of information-bearing pattern in the environment of the new creation" (Polkinghorne and Beale, 2009). Yes, this is why Church supports the pro-life campaign; as soon as the newly formed zygote nests in the maternal uterus has a unique DNA, it has a soul. And yes, if Christ is not risen, our faith is futile; we are still in our sins! *"Then also those who have fallen asleep in Christ have perished"* (*1 Corinthians 15:17-18*).

Let's see now: We know that there is a Master of the Universe and we are in continuous interdependence on Him. We know that we have a soul, and this has an eternal life which follows after our limited earthly life is over. We know that the soul's efficient growth and existence can be accomplished only in relation with the Master of the Universe who controls everything. Therefore, the only way for our soul to act is by being in a permanent dialogue with Him, a dialogue which proves vital but at the same time has to be as simple and rich as possible. This is **the Prayer** that Malorussian monk, Saint Paisius Velichkovsky, who resided for a short while at Mount Athos and then for much longer on the ancient Romanian territory, searched for the key of practicing this prayer. Eventually, after he found the most concise and powerful formula of it, he intensely practiced it, and enclosed this practice with the personal example of his life. "In the catacombs, the most frequent image is the figure of a woman in prayer, the *Orant*; she represents the one true attitude of the human soul. It is not enough to say prayers; one must become, be prayer, prayer incarnate", Paul Evdokimov wrote (Evdokimov, 1985). Saint Paisius Velichkovsky of Neamts was such a person. We should learn the power of prayer and make it our weapon against the evil's temptations and our ladder of spiritual ascent. Saint Paisius offers us a treasure of knowledge about real prayer, resulting from the Holy Fathers' experience through the *Philocalia*, and also from his own experience. This is the first part of the answer to our introductory question of why we should study the life of Saint Paisius.

There is continuity throughout the whole history of the mankind that regards the interaction between the Lord and the human being in its profound structure. The faith and trust in the Creator and Master of the

Universe provides fresh strength repeatedly to the weary man. Let us have in our heart and mind the words of a beautiful prayer heard in Church: "O God, Who renew the world through mysteries beyond all telling, grant, we pray, that Your church and Christian people may be guided by Your eternal design and not be deprived by Your help in this challenging present age." Awareness of the increased and specific potential dangers of today's world ravaged by evil is important.

Such a thought leads to the second part of the answer to the question this Foreword started with. It was brought up by the Fathers from Saint Herman of Alaska Monastery. The remarkable Christian work done by Saint Paisius and his disciples in Eastern Europe represents a genuine Age of Faith, which is in total contrast to the Age of Reason proclaimed in Western Europe by its contemporary, irreligious works and philosophy of the Enlightenment Movement by Voltaire, Jean-Jacques Rousseau, and Denis Diderot. Paisianism has remained a firm response to the Apostacy that has intensified in our present time. By keeping alive the profound teachings and the example of the existences of all the Fathers during Christian history, and by being themselves a philokalic, ardent Prayer, the Paisianists bear an incommensurable, inner power that unknowingly counterbalances the damages produced by evil in our world.

Finally, the third part of the answer to the question first posed in this Foreword is Saint Paisius' great contribution to the monastic world that embodies the secret, spiritual engine of humanity. If this engine does not run well humanity suffers deeply. As Father Cleopa

Ilie said, Blessed Paisius of Neamts was the wisest Abbot from all the Abbots of the Romanian monasteries since the eighteenth century until current times, and his great personality is beloved and respected by all the Orthodox countries for his monastic qualities of father, teacher, adviser, confessor and sleepless praying intercessor. Father Cleopa listed the following unique virtues that Saint Paisius had and transmitted to others: the holiness of his life, the ceaseless prayer of the heart, the humility and obedience, the participation at all the religious services, the daily confession and communion, the canonic rules in the monastic cells, the love for the others. "All these virtues," concluded Father Cleopa, "combined with the grace of the Holy Spirit, are able to transform the heart, to unite the monk to Christ and to ensure the salvation of the soul" (see Cleopa Ilie, 2012 and Bălan, 2001).

We might ask what connection exists between the monastic principles mentioned above and the actual our own lives as laymen. Saint John Climacus has an answer: "Some people living carelessly in the world put a question to me: 'How can we, who are married and living amid public cares, aspire to the monastic life?' I answered, 'Do whatever good you may. Speak evil to no one. Rob no one. Tell no lie. Despise no one and carry no hate. Do not separate yourself from the church assemblies. Show compassion to the needy. Do not be a cause of scandal to anyone. Stay away from the bed of another, and be satisfied with what your own wives can provide you. If you do this, you are not far from the Kingdom of Heaven" (St. John Climacus,

1982). We also can keep in mind Father Roman Braga's notice that "Man is the 'theandric mode' of existence in which God and nature must be combined in a harmonious synthesis" and the monks who might theoretically represent earthly angels among us can inspire us with their model of striving for that harmony (Braga, 1997). "Monks and married people, the diamond-cutters of heavenly stones" with their "chastity bring creation to perfection" (Evdokimov, 1985).

Father Seraphim Rose in the introduction to the Biography of Saint Paisius written by Metrophanes, quoted the words of Elder Macarius of Optina a Paisian Father of nineteenth century: "The holy God-bearing Fathers wrote about great spiritual gifts not so that anyone might strive indiscriminately to receive them, but so that those who do not have them, hearing about such exalted gifts and revelations which were received by those who were worthy, might acknowledge their own profound infirmity and great insufficiency, and might involuntarily be inclined to humility, which is more necessary for those seeking salvation than all other works and virtues" (see Metrophanes, 1994).

By God's mysterious will, the commemoration day of Saint Paisius, known for his ascetic life and unextinguishable thirst for the Divine, coincides with the first day of the preparatory Lent for the Holy Nativity of the Lord. It is an important feast for the Romanian monasticism and for the whole Orthodox monastic world. For sure, this coincidence carries a profound message for all of us. In fact, God works in various, mysterious and wise ways. By his life, Saint Paisius ties the Orthodox places of deep faith where he has been: Ukraine, Moldavia, Walachia, Mount Athos. By his writings and disciples, he ties further the Orthodox Romania, Russia, Alaska and the rest of United States. "Rejoice, Blessed Paisius, sacred bridge to the Holy Fathers", says repeatedly the Akathist Hymn dedicated to him (see *The Bicentennial of St. Paisius Velichkovsky*, 1994b). As the Psalmist David says, thinking of the saints of God on earth, "*in them He magnified all His will*" (*Psalm 15/16:3*).

This book is part of an initial project about the Sacred Time of Our Life, based on a previous book published in Romanian language in 2006 entitled "Treptele de văzduh ale sufletului și setea de Dumnezeu", i.e. in English free translation "The Ladder of the Inner Sky and the Thirst for God" or in verbatim translation "The Pneumatological Stages of the Soul and the Yearning Desire for the Godhead" (Groza, 2006). Three separate books resulted from this project: "Discovering the Sacred Time of Our Life" about the general principles of the Orthodox Christianity (2016), "Living the Sacred Time of Our Life" about the implementation of all principles in our concrete Christian life (2018), and the present book "Saint Paisius Velichkovsky and Paisianism" which with its three major elements – Jesus Prayer, Philokalia and Saint Paisius, the Saint who embodied them, comes as a corollary uniting through Paisianism the whole Orthodox world.

*

Acknowledgments. I thank very much Father Archimandrite Mark Melone in Laurence, Massachusetts, Fathers Ian McKinnon and Dane Popovich in

California, and Fathers Anthony Michaels and Vladimir Lecko in Wisconsin, for their precious suggestions; the recently departed Father Petronius Tanase from Mount Athos and writer Vasile Andru from Romania for their trust and moral support; Cary O'Keeffe, my first reader, for her excellent help in the editing work and for her gracious and vital help in making clearer this book's message; and my family and friends for their continuous love and encouragement.

Introduction

With his methodical reasoning Saint Thomas Aquinas viewed Saint Barnabas as "*a good man, full of the Holy Spirit and of faith*" (*Acts 11:24*). St. Barnabas was also a companion of Saint Paul in his missionary work. Thinking of him Saint Thomas wrote, "Two things are necessary for a man - interior perfection (1) and exterior conversation (2), the first for himself, the second for his neighbor.

Interior perfection is in two parts, knowledge of truth (1.1) and love of goodness (1.2). The first is perfection of the intellect, the second the fullness of all the affections. Exterior conversation consists in two things, acts of usefulness (2.1) and gravity of manners (2.2). These four are indicated in these words of commendation of Barnabas - illumination of mind, inflammation of love, utility in action, and a serious way of life" (see Every et al., 1984).

Saint Paisius of Neamts (Velichkovsky) did not travel for missionary purposes like Saint Barnabas, but he combined all of the latter's virtues. In the monasteries where he was Abbot, he had disciples of many nationalities. His life was dedicated entirely to the Lord. He said often that if we put our hope in God, even if we live a day and then we die, it is much more worthwhile than to live very many years but with doubts in our soul.

CHRISTIAN INNER SOLITUDE. Historically Pentecost marked the beginning of Christianity for the Jewish people. In the year 49 A.D. the Apostolic Synod gathered in Jerusalem (*Acts 15:1-33*) and established the requirements for the non-Judaic people, the Gentiles, in order to be accepted as Christians. The Word of God spread in the world. Christianity became a spiritual power that the tyrants learned to fear. In the year 64 the fool emperor Nero burned two thirds of Rome and started the campaign of persecution against the Christians. The second large period of persecution was in the years 81-96 under the emperor Domitian. Until the edict of indulgence issued by the emperor Galerius in 311 and especially the Edict of Milan, the letter of religious toleration signed by the emperors Constantine and Licinius, Christianity experienced oppression, prison, torture, and martyrdom. Hiding in catacombs and other covert places became common in the first two Christian centuries.

Some individuals, stronger in spirit and more ardent in faith, burned by the thirst of uniting with God, retired in the desert areas trying to imitate the ascetic life of Saint John the Baptist and, much more, to undergo forty days of fasting and prayer to Jesus. *"Behold, I fled far away, and lodged in the wilderness. I wait for the One who saves me from faintheartedness and storm"* (*Psalm 54/55:8-9*). The persecution edict of the emperor Decius in 250 intensified this trend. Without being named as hermits, they were mentioned in some early writings. In the year 250 Saint Paul of Thebes, who is considered the first Christian hermit or anchorite as he was described by Saint Jerome, ensembled the first community of eremitic monks in the Thebaidic desert of Superior Egypt. Despite the fact that the hermits strived in an ascetic life in remote places far from any human congregation, they were still relatively close to each other. Therefore "loose-knit" monastic communities became possible. After Saint Anthony the Great completely withdrew from the civilized world, he established in the year 270, based on this kind of *solitary monasticism* (the Greek word "eremos" means "desert"), the first ever two Christian monasteries within which the anchorites communicated with each other, sharing experience and prayers.

A big relief affected the multitudes after the Christian faith became public and tolerated. However, some people feared the important potential risk of mixing the Christian principles with worldly things, of introducing pagan habits or concepts into the Christian precepts, and of creating heresies and misinterpretations, which could cause major deterioration or even desecration. Strong believers like Saint Macarius of Egypt felt that the influx of new converts who brought with them a profane attitude into the church caused a real distraction from a life of deep and powerful prayer. He looked for the isolation of the desert, where the complete solitude would make the dialogue with God his exclusive material and spiritual food. In the desert he could concentrate the thoughts of his mind and the feelings of his heart only on the Heavenly Kingdom.

Saint Macarius of Egypt is one of the first teachers of pure prayer, prayer which in time would be taken over by the other Holy Fathers under the name of Jesus Prayer. He said one day, "There is no need to waste time with words; it is enough to hold out our hands and say, 'Lord, according to your desire and to your wisdom, have mercy.' For such a focused prayer, strength of the spirit is needed and no distraction from outside" (see Kallistos, 1986). On the other hand, physical sacrifice, as the previously mentioned martyrdom, remained a spiritual necessity for the real devouts. However, because they were not strong enough to withdraw like the hermits, lacking the physical ability and inner firmness for a completely solitary existence, they still needed the stimulative force of living, praying and worshipping together. Therefore, their defensive reaction led to the formation of another type of monachal life: *coenobitic monasticism*. Historians consider the Jewish communities of Essenes (throughout Roman Judeea) and Therapeutae (spread in diaspora, mainly next to Alexandria) which flourished before Christ's time up to first century AD, as the precursors of the coenobitic monasteries. Saint Macarius of Egypt, also known as Saint Macarius the Great, grouped together anchorites in the desert between Nitria and Scetis and established a monachal life in the years 328-330.

The monks lived in separate cells, keeping the "innermost desert" but gathering for regular religious services on Saturdays and Sundays. The first *real* coenobitic Christian monasteries, where the monks lived together in a solidary unit, organized according to strict rules, were constituted by Saint Pachomius in 346 at Tabenna, in Egypt, on the Superior Nile. The monks lived in rooms, shared belongings, worked, ate and worshipped together. They had a wise, older leader named Abbot (Starets). They strived for virtues by cultivating humility and obedience.

The Egyptian Patericon (see *Patericul* 1999a and *The Lives of the Egyptian Desert Fathers*, 1975), a well-known writing about the experience and teachings of the ascetic inhabitants of these places, became besides the Bible and the Ladder of Saint John Climacus one of the three main books for everybody belonging to the eremitic or coenobitic monastic systems. Later, Saint Basil the Great (329-379) for the Eastern Church and Saint John Cassian (360-435, native of Scythia Minor on the ancient Romanian territory) for the Western Church wrote the principles of the coenobitic life which became a guiding rule for the following centuries of monasticism. Saints Augustine (354-430) and Saint Benedict (480-547) developed further coenobitic communities in the West.

The presence of the monasteries somewhere on the globe is an often ignored but vital, spiritual support for the whole humanity. An American nun noticed that today in Romania (and like that it is in the whole Eastern Europe, including Russia where the monastic communities and priests were persecuted by the communist regime more than seven decades), "village and monastic life are deeply intertwined.

Villagers love their monasteries, and make regular pilgrimages to them, especially during the four Fasts, so that they can confess and receive the Holy Mysteries. No matter how poor they are, they never come to the monastery without bringing something to give. It may even be a few potatoes from their crop. And, likewise, the monasteries consider their faithful people to be the wealth, the jewels of their country, and when the people come to the monastery on pilgrimage, the monasteries serve them as if they are Christ

Himself" (Nun Nina, 1995). A different philosophy prevails in the West where people are more materialistic and the percentage of unbelievers is much bigger. However, an elevating and highly emotional case, documented by a beautiful film, can inspire everybody regardless of the intensity of faith.

Despite the fact that their monastery was beloved by the local population which participated regularly at the majority of the religious services, the Cistercian monks of the Monastery of Diepenveen in Netherlands decided in 2015 to leave the initial 120-monk monastic building and farm unit that had been set up hundred-thirty years ago. One reason was that it became too big of a place for the remainder of less than a dozen monks, but the main reason was that it reached too large popularity and it was too frequently visited by laymen, in conflict with the desire of the monks who needed a quiet, undisturbed way of life, focused on continuous worship and individual prayer. They moved to Schiermonnikoog, a remote Dutch island, with sand dunes. Asked if the monasteries still play a role in the present society and are of any use, they answered that the use is the simple idea that *they are there*, that they exist. "For many people the fact that we are here is a very clear signal. That we should not give up prayers. That God remains alive in this society. That He does not have to be stored or hidden because He is still there." The name of this documentary TV film is *Schiermonnikoog (The Island of the Monks),* and was written and directed by Anne-Christine Girardot for to the Dutch KRO-NCRV network (https://kloosterschiermonnikoog.nl/english/).

JESUS PRAYER. The main focus in monasteries is always on (**a**) serving God with worship, fasting and prayer, (**b**) the podvig as an unseen war against the temptations and (**c**) growing virtues among which humility, purity and love are the main ones. During a deeply silent night at Mount Athos, when far above heavy clusters of stars were hanging in the sky and far below the waves of the sea were moving with a hardly perceptible whisper, the Abbot of Saint Anna's Skete asked the thrilled Romanian poet Sandu Tudor when at the time remote sounds of bells and wood semantrons started to be heard from the monasteries and sketes of the mountain, "Where were you, brother Sandu, at this hour back home in Bucharest?"

The question struck like a hammer. The poet tried to chase away the images that were haunting his soul – bars, nightclubs, cabarets, literature café, pubs, bohemian hours, foolish things, affairs. He did not answer. The Abbot said with a gentle, low voice, "We, here at Athos, believe that the Lord saves the world because of the monks and hermits' prayers and vigils." This is the actual support of our world: the unceasing prayers of the monks for all of us, even if they do not say specific names of persons.

Thinking of Our Lord Jesus Christ, the Son of God, every Christian has in mind a multitude of vital and important concepts, especially those of a very profound significance like incarnation, crucifixion, resurrection, and ascension (see Staniloae, 1980). Orthodox spirituality has formulated a short and simple phrase that became the core of the Christian's prayer life. It contains all the deep meanings resulted from the act of contemplating Divine Person of Christ and of following His teachings. This prayer formula has been elaborated and enriched by the personal spiritual experience of the Holy Fathers over more than nine centuries. By incorporating it in the breathing rhythm, in the inner intimacy of the body, mind and heart, the continuous state of prayer becomes achievable, accomplishing the "pray without ceasing" task given by Saint Paul (*1 Thessalonians 5:17*). Saint Seraphim of Sarov reminded us Saint Isaac the Syrian's words, "Without uninterrupted prayer we cannot draw near to God" (see Belonick, 1998).

This short prayer is called the "Jesus Prayer" and it succeeds by using the extraordinary invocative power of Jesus Christ's name to gather in only twelve words the mysteries of incarnation, transfiguration and sacrifice, the mysteries of the double nature of Christ and of the unity of the Holy Trinity, and the elements of a Christian life including veneration and salvation. The prayer takes its power mainly from two names: the name Jesus that comes from the Greek word *Iēsous* in Greek (*Yehoshua* in Hebrew) and means "Savior," and the name Christ that comes from *Christos* in Greek and means "the anointed one" or "the chosen by God"; the latter name translates the Hebrew word *Meshiach* or Messiah (see Un moine de l'Église d'Orient, 1963; Kallistos, 1986; Groza, 2016).

The words of the blind man from Jericho prefigure, in a way, the Jesus Prayer. He cried unceasingly, "*Jesus, son of David, have mercy on me!*" (*Luke 18:38*), as Jesus was approaching Jericho on His way to Jerusalem for Palm Sunday. Taught by the Holy Fathers, we pray saying, "**Lord Jesus Christ, Son of God, have mercy on me, a sinner.**" The first Holy

Father who clearly suggested a coherent expression of the Jesus Prayer, together with the method of saying it, was Saint Symeon the New Theologian (949-1022), who had the vision of heavenly light and of his spirit being separated from his body when he was fourteen years old (see Princess Ileana of Romania, 1959). Because of the greatness and the extraordinary depth of his spiritual writings, Saint Symeon was often likened to the author of the fourth Gospel, Saint Apostle and Evangelist John, the Theologian. The Jesus Prayer that reunites the mind, heart, and spirit into a unique effort of deification, became then the major focus of the hesychasm. The goal of the precepts of this spiritual movement is the profound inward concentration necessary for an effective dialogue with Christ, which unfolds in a complete silence, deep peace, and indescribable joy.

The Jesus Prayer's sentence "embodies the two chief mysteries of the Christian faith, the Incarnation and the Trinity" (Kallistos, 1986). As the same Bishop Kallistos of Diokletia (Timothy Ware) emphasized, the great efficacy of Jesus Prayer resides on two aspects: the power of the Name and the discipline of repetition incorporated in the body's rhythm of breathing. Regarding the first aspect, the overwhelming power of Jesus' name was frequently emphasized by the Holy Scripture. The angel told Joseph, *"And she will bring forth a son, and you shall call His name JESUS, for He will save His people from their sins"* (*Matthew 1:21*). Saint Paul wrote, *"Therefore God also has highly exalted Him and given Him the name which is above every name, that at the <u>name of Jesus</u> every knee should bow, of those in heaven, and of those on earth,* *and of those under the earth, and that every tongue should confess that Jesus Christ is Lord, to the glory of God the Father"* (*Philippians 2:9-11*). Our Lord, Jesus Christ, said to His disciples, *"Whatever you ask the Father <u>in My name</u> He will give You*" (*John 16:23*). One might say that, actually, the Jesus Prayer forms the spinal cord of the entire Orthodox faith. The Romanian theologian and philosopher Nichifor Crainic considered it "the core of Orthodoxy" (see Un moine de l'Église d'Orient, 1963). By the mysterious and wise work of God, the existence of Saint Paisius Velichkovsky of Neamts helped tye together the Holy Orthodox Fathers of Eastern Europe and the Middle East on one hand and Orthodoxy in America on the other, linking harmoniously saints, peoples and places within the larger world of Orthodox Christianity. The secret substance of this tight connection is the practice of the Jesus Prayer, also called the Prayer of the Mind or the Prayer of the Heart, according to the spiritual level achieved.

PHILOKALIA. The Philokalia is a Greek collection compiled in the eighteenth century by Saints Nikodemos of Mount Athos and Macarios of Corinth. It contains teachings about saying the Jesus Prayer which come from the texts written by the Holy Fathers of the fourth to fifteenth centuries. The title word is composed of *philia* "love" and *kallos* "beauty", which means "love of the beautiful, the exalted, [and] the good" (Coniaris, 1998). The term was firstly used by Saints Basil and Gregory of Nazianz for their antology made of Origene's texts (Jean Gouillard's preface to *Petite Philocalie de la prière du coeur*, 1979). There is a place in the Old Testament where Christ, "the Beloved One", is addressed with the following words: "*You are more beautiful than the sons of men; Grace was poured out on Your lips; Therefore, God blessed You forever*" (*Psalm 44/45:3*). The whole Psalm is considered as a "prophetic description of the Word incarnate," where symbolic words name the Mother of God, the Church, and the Gentiles (see *The Orthodox Study Bible*, footnote on page 711). The Serbian Bishop Nicolai Velimirovic, nicknamed the New Chrysostom, commented that here "David is not speaking of the physical beauty of Christ the King but of His spiritual, divine beauty." Saint Gregory of Nyssa wrote about Christ, "You alone are an icon of Eternal beauty," and added that we might "become what He is, imitating Him Who shines within" us. The great Russian writer Fyodor Dostoyevsky considered that "beauty will save the world" (for all three quotations see Coniaris, 1998).

Saint Macarios prepared the first text of Philokalia at Mount Athos in 1777 and Saint Nicodemos made additions, especially for Introduction and Lives of the Fathers. The Prince of Moldavia John Mavrocordatos supported financially the publication which took place in Venice in 1782. The book, written in Greek, put together the teachings of over thirty Fathers. Among them are Evagrius of Pontus, Nilus of Ancyra, Diadochus of Photice, Maximus the Confessor, John Damascene, Philoteus the Sinaite, Symeon the New Theologian, Nicephorus the Monk, Kallistos and Ignatius Xanthopoulos, Gregory the Sinaite, Gregory Palamas, and John of Carpathos (see *Petite Philocalie de la prière du coeur*, 1979; Coniaris, 1998).

Saint Nicodemos calls the Philokalia "the bread of knowledge and wisdom," and also "the wine that spiritually delights the heart and dispels all the material and immaterial things because of deification." For some people the Philokalia is "a living out of the Bible" (see Coniaris, 1998). The Philokalia is not intended only for the monastic world but also for the laity because as Father Anthony M. Coniaris justly wrote, the Orthodox Church gives to all of us seven great legacies: the baptism, the sacraments, the apostolic faith, prayer, the Divine Liturgy, the Holy Scripture, and the Philokalia. He summarized the points touched by the rich depth of the Philokalia: the passions, the battle with the temptations, the ceaseless watch for protecting the mind and heart, the state of prayer and the Jesus Prayer, humility, the purification of heart, the true wisdom as a goal ("when the heart has acquired stillness it will perceive the heights and depth of knowledge"), and the union with Christ, as a supreme destination achieved through love (Coniaris, 1998).

Saint Paisius Velichkovsky was the author of the earliest translation from Greek of "The Philokalia" (1793). He accomplished his important work in Moldavia, at Neamts Monastery, a site that became at the end of the eighteenth century a center of Orthodox spirituality equal in importance with Mount Sinai in the sixth century and Mount Athos in the eleventh through fourteenth centuries (Crainic, 1993).

The Slavonic translation of Saint Paisius spread fast in Russia under the name of "Dobrotolijubie." It was printed at Saint-Petersburg in 1793 and gained such popularity that it was reprinted eight times. It constituted the favored spiritual food of the Russian monastic world of the nineteenth century besides the Bible and the Great Monologue of Dmitry of Rostov (see the Preface at *Petite Philocalie de la prière du coeur*, 1979). The very important, large monastic centers Valaam and Optino used it intensely. A Romanian version was created in 1807.

Saint Ignatius Bryanchaninov, Bishop of the Caucasus and the Black Sea, made another Russian version in 1857. Later, between 1876 and 1890, Saint Theophanes the Recluse reorganized the material, eliminated some texts, added others and published a five-volume Philokalia. Based on this, the famous book "The Way of a Pilgrim" about the Jesus Prayer was issued at Optina Monastery talking about the only possible way to make accomplishable what Saint Paul urged his disciples and, through them, all the Christians to do: *"pray without ceasing"* (*1 Thessalonians 5:17*). The Pilgrim's book spread fast in the whole Orthodox world of Eastern Europe (the Romanian title was "Journey to Heaven") but also in the different world of Western Europe (the French title was "Récits d'un Pèlerine Russe").

The third Philokalia translation, the largest so far, in 12 volumes, containing over forty authors, was done from Greek in Romanian by Father Dumitru Staniloae in the years 1946-1991 (Editura Institutului Biblic şi de Misiune Ortodoxă, Bucureşti). He included teachings from the Elders of the Romanian hesychasm in the eighth volume, besides the other Holy Fathers' teachings. Father Staniloae worked under the very oppressive conditions of the atheist communist regime. Due to the anti-religious campaign of the government Father Staniloae was in prison in the period of 1958-1963.

The first volume was published in 1946 and in a larger number of copies in 1947, but after that the authorities stopped the publication of the others. The volumes II - IV were illegally printed in 1947-1948 and circulated unbound amoung the readers with the risk of prison. In 1976-1980 religious persecution decreased and the author published volumes V-IX.

In 1951 E. Kadloubovsky and G.E.H. Palmer, two students of the Russian esotericist Pyotr Ouspensky, finished the first English translation of an abbreviated version of the Philokalia, based on a previous Russian translation; it was entitled "Writings from the Philokalia on Prayer of the Heart" (Faber and Faber, London). Along the same lines, in 1953 Jean Gouillard made an abbreviated version in French entitled "Petite Philocalie de la Priere du Coeur," based on the Greek texts (Éditions des Cahiers du Sud, Marseille). Later, in 1957-1963, a larger version was issued in English in five volumes as a result of the work of G.E.H. Palmer, Philip Sherrard, and Kallistos Ware; they followed entirely the original writing of Saint Nikodemos in Greek (Faber and Faber, London). Other translations have been made in French, German, Italian, Spanish, Finnish and Arabic languages.

1. Saint Paisius Velichkovsky of Neamts
1.1. Life of Saint Paisius

The most renowned and published biography of Saint Paisius Velichkovky of Neamts (1722-1794) was written by the schema-monk Metrophanes from Dragomirna Monastery, one of the three Romanian monasteries where the Saint was Abbot. This monk was a long-time disciple of the elder and a hard worker in hand-copying manuscripts. He started to write the elder's life in Russian in 1814 at the request of the Abbot Sylvester (see Metrophanes, 1976). Later four more Romanians wrote Saint Paisius' biography (this time in Romanian): Reader Brother Isaac, Reader Brother Gregory (tonsured in monasticism by Saint Paisius in 1790 and raised later as Metropolitan Gregory IV of Walachia), Schema-monk Platon, and Monk Kiriac the Confessor.

At the request of his disciples Saint Paisius wrote an autobiography which remained unfinished. It covers the period from his birth (1722) up to the end of his staying at the Romanian Sketes Trăisteni and Cârnu (1745). A very good book, published in Romanian, contains the autobiography and Saint Paisius life stories written by schema-monk Metrophanes, Vitalius the Monk and Gregory the Reader. It also contains excerpts from an introductory study by the Italian priest Elia Citterio, the burial sermon written by Isaac the Reader, the religious service for Saint Paisius held regularly at Neamts and Secoul Monasteries, and the rules of monastic life at the three monasteries that Saint Paisius shepherded (see *Cuviosul Paisie de la Neamț...*, 2002). As Elia Citterio commented in his quoted introductory study, Saint Paisius did not emphasize in the autobiography his own spiritual struggle and achievements but all the dramatic events he had to go through, which he gathered in an educational and inspiring story describing the difficulties a young person, thirsty for a life in Christ, has to face and overcome.

THE FIRST YEARS OF SAINT PAISIUS' LIFE.
Saint Paisius Velichkovsky was born on December 21, 1722, in Poltava, in the part of Ukraine occupied by the Russian Empire. Poltava, located 200 miles southeast of Kyiv (Kiev), is the historic place where the Russian tzar Peter I's army won a bloody battle against the Swedish king Charles' forces in 1709 and from where King Charles escaped into Bendery, Moldavia.

The name of the newborn, the eleventh of twelve children in their Malorussian family, was Pyotr. His father, Ivan Velichkovsky, reposed when Pyotr was 4 years old. He had served as Archpriest of Poltava, like his grandfather Luke Velichkovsky. They both worshiped in the same cathedral – the Dormition of Theotokos' Cathedral, and both were its rectors. The great-grandfather, Simeon, was a rich, well-known Cossak. Pyotr's mother, Irina, was the daughter of the rich and respected Jewish merchand Mandea who by baptism into the Orthodox Church changed his name to Gregory Mandenko. Later Saint Paisius' mother entered the monastery under the name Nun Juliana. Pyotr was a very shy, introspect, quiet boy, so quiet that his mother very rarely heard him speak. He went to school early, together with his younger brother Theodor. In two years, he learned to read so well that the Holy Scripture, the Lives of Saints, the writings of Saints Ephraim the Syrian, Doroteus and John Chrysostom gradually became his favorites. His brother Theodor reposed when Pytor was seven years old. In the meantime, Pyotr's older brother Ivan was ordained a priest and five years later he began serving as an Archpriest in the same Cathedral with his father and grandfather. When Pyotr reached the age of 13, his brother Ivan Velichkovsky reposed. Pyotr's mother, her brother Vasily Mandenko, and Pyotr's godfather Vasily Vasilevich Kochubey decided to go to the Metropolitan of Kyiv and ask him to officially certify that when Pyotr became a priest he would retain the same job as his grandfather, father and older brother in the same parish and Cathedral. The Metropolitan made the document but asked the boy to study at the high school of the Kyiv Theological Academy, founded in 1633 by the Metropolitan of Romanian (Moldavian) origin Petru Movila.

Gifted with a great love for reading and praying, Pyotr studied there three years. Being in Kyiv he had the chance to visit the local Lavra of the Caves which he liked very much. Pretty soon, despite being a good and hard-working student, Pyotr started to long for a monastic life. At the age of only fourteen, he already understood the essence of Christian living: he loved his neighbor, was humble, and did not judge anybody

(Joantă, 1992). "Seeking to know what passes knowledge" (Akathist, Kontakion 2, in *The bicentennial of St. Paisius Velichkovsky*, 1994b), he talked with his friends and decided to enter monastic life. He asked the elders at Kitaev Skete, a place he loved, to be accepted but hearing that this contradicted his mother's will they declined the request because, according to the civil laws of the day, she had the power to come with the local authorities and remove him from the skete, which would cause a great disturbance. Therefore, they advised him to look for a place where no such interdiction could function.

Pyotr continued with the fourth year of studies at the Academy. It happened that one day he attended the Divine Liturgy at the Kyiv Metropolitan' Palace Kudreavetz. The service was celebrated by the Metropolitan of Moldavia Anthony with his assistants. The Metropolitan was a refugee that time, due to the Russian-Turkish war lasting from 1735-1739; he had served as Archbishop at Chernigov. Pyotr was delighted. He developed a sudden and lasting love for the Romanian language and the people speaking it. Consequently, he decided to cross the border at the first opportunity into Moldo-Vlachia, where "the holy monasteries adorned the sites like the stars in the sky," as the biographer Reader Gregory wrote (Zamfirescu, 1996). Pyotr talked about crossing the border with his good friend Dmitry and made a plan. Unfortunately, he got sick, so Dmitry had to go alone to Kyiv to find out the best way to get out. As soon as Pyotr recovered they prepared for the journey. Dmitry wanted to say goodbye first to his mother. Pyotr knew that their mothers would not agree to their leaving. His own mother, Irina Velichkovsky, dreamed for a different destiny for her son who was the only child who remained alive from her twelve children. She wanted him to marry, to continue the Velichkovsky lineage and to become a priest at the Dormition Cathedral. Pyotr asked for his mother's blessing and promised in a vague way that he would attend the school later. Dmitry met firm opposition from his mother, so Pyotr had to look for another companion. He found a priest's son who wanted to visit his father in Novgorod-Seversky and the route was through Chernigov where Pyotr planned to go.

The two youngsters hired an old man to take them in his frail little boat on the Desna River upstream to Chernigov. There they hoped to contact the hieromonk Pachomius, a good friend of the Metropolitan of Moldavia, for instructions about their much-dreamed journey to Moldavia. Pyotr suffered very much during this trip. Due to his light clothes he shivered unceasingly from cold. His fragile body could barely keep pace with his friend in paddling the boat.

Unlike his travelmates he caught lice which bothered and weakened him. Even more so, Pyotr feared every minute that they would sink because only a few inches separated the edge of the boat from the surface of the water, and many times the wind or the current produced big waves. Unfortunately, he was correct to be afraid, but God saved them miraculously from drowning in a powerful vortex of the river. At Oster somebody saw their boat and realized how insecure they were and what a slight chance they had to make it all the way to Chernigov. So, he took them all in his big, strong lotka but another event struck and threatened their life: a huge portion of the shore collapsed over them. Again, miraculously, they survived. Arrived at Chernigov, the two teenagers visited Father Pachomius who advised them to go to hiero-schema-monk Joaquim at Liubetzky Monastery, located on the left bank of Dnieper River. He also could help them to cross the river into the Ukrainian zone occupied by Polish-Lithuanian Commonwealth, which helped them avoid problems with the guards.

The two travelers covered the long distance to Liubech and avoided the city, walking straight towards the monastery. However, to their great despair, soldiers stopped them. But the Lord directed an old monk to pass by, who told the guards that the young men were apprentices and the guards let them go. The Abbot welcomed the two visitors and immediately gave them tasks to fulfil. Pyotr had to distribute food items from storage to the people in the kitchen. He barely managed to handle the heavy barrels and wooden boxes because of his fragile body, but he never complained and loved his Abbot with all his heart. Somebody gave him Saint John Climacus' book *The Ladder of Divine Ascent*, and he proceeded to copy by hand half of it in the evenings in the poor, dim light of the smoky rushlight that was regularly used by the monks. Every time the gradually-thickening cloud of smoke cumulated under the ceiling reached a level lower than his head, Pyotr had to open the little window, go out of the cell and wait a long while until the smoke dissipated. Then he reentered the cell, closed the window and resumed writing until a new dense layer of smoke covered his head. Fortunately, the administrator eventually gave him an oil lamp which made everything easier.

RASOPHORE IN THE FOREIGN LAND. After the old Abbot of Liubetzky Monastery died, a new, despotic, young abbot replaced him. Pyotr was deeply disappointed and decided to leave the monastery and to cross the border into the foreign Polish-Lithuanian-Ukrainian land. He did that in the sixth week of Great Lent on a moonlit night with a friend, running between two guard points over the frozen Dnieper River. They headed to Chernobyl through unending forest, sleeping in villages along the way. On their journey they had to cross Pripyat, a smaller river, whose ice was much thinner and partially cracked. Miraculously they made it to the other shore without drowning. With tears of gratitude in their eyes they thanked God when, scared to death by a sudden deafening roar, looked back and saw that the whole ice cover cracked and huge slabs of ice rushed down the river. They made it that very day to the town of Chernobyl. It was Lazarus' Saturday. In town, they unexpectedly met a neighbor from Poltava who told Pyotr that his mother had gotten sick, and she was weeping unconsoled that she had lost her son.

With their hearts burdened with sadness for their families but filled with hope for a secluded life devoted completely to God, the two young people continued to travel. Pyotr had never walked so much in his entire life. His left sole and ankle swelled and his whole left leg hurt. He could barely step while placing the weight of his body on his heels, and he frequently stopped for short rests. His companion was exasperated and many times wanted to leave him in pain and to continue the journey alone. Pyotr tearfully begged his companion not to abandon him in the middle of the woods. They started now to halt more often in villages for one or two days to allow Pyotr's leg to rest. The trip became an endless nightmare until one day when, as he wrote in his autobiography, Pyotr felt the Lord's unspoken mercy descend upon him and the pain disappeared, the leg returned to its normal shape and healed, he could walk lightly and easily.

They reached the little skete Rjishtev, on the right bank of Dnieper. This was downstream from Kyiv which was located on the opposite bank in the Russian Ukraine. Despite being now on Polish-controlled Ukrainian land, the skete still belonged to the Kirilovsky Monastery in Kyiv, as it had been for a long time. Imediately after asking for the blessing of the elders and a little place to rest Pyotr fell down, sick to his stomach. For an entire month he suffered, becoming extremely weak and losing the ability to walk. He kept tirelessly praying with great fervor to God to save him because he did not want to die in that place. By God's mercy it happened that three foreign monks who were heading to Moldavia showed up for a short while at the skete. Pyotr asked them to let him go with them into that "blessed country" but they hesitated because of his terrible weakness. Eventually they left together. The trail passed a mountain and the climbing proved to be agony for Pyotr's poor body. Fortunately, they soon descended into a large, flat, smooth plain with refreshing air and he regained gradually his lifeforce. He thanked the Lord from his soul's depth and resumed walking joyously. However, another trial waited for him on the road. A frightening thunder storm with hail and tons of water ravaged the plain, covering the ground with hazelnut-sized ice balls. The monks ran fast to shelter themselves but Pyotr remained in the rain moving with great difficulty. He didn't reach the village until late at night where he asked for overnight shelter.

Soon they came to the Moshinsky Mountains where they decided to split up: the monks continued their trip to Moldavia and Pyotr rested a couple of days at the Ascension of the Lord's Monastery, one of the few monasteries in those mountains. He heard about the God-pleasing old hermit Isichia living hidden in the area and begged a hieromonk to guide him there. Fortunately, the ascetic man, diligent in following the Lord's spiritual commandments, was not bothered by his visit, welcomed him with love and enriched his young heart with many wise words, which "*more to be desired*" were "*than gold and a very precious stone, sweeter also than honey and the honey comb*" (*Psalm 18/19:11*). Pyotr was deeply impressed by the hermit's ardor and zeal for the Divinity's mercy, when he heard that the old man greatly desired a rare piece of the Holy Fathers' writing for spiritual improvement and despite all risks and dangers, he walked over thirteen hundred miles to a skete in a remote mountain area beyond Chernigov to get it. After long, insistent, desperate supplications, the hermit was allowed to borrow the manuscript he considered to be a real treasure of teachings necessary to the podvig required by the salvation of the soul. He left the skete, walked back the whole distance to his cell, worked hard to copy the manuscript and then he returned it, disregarding the great efforts of repeating such a tiring, unsafe journey. The anchorite's eyes weakened very much after copying numerous manuscripts from Holy Fathers' teachings. Pyotr hoped to be accepted by the old hermit as a disciple but in his great humility the latter refused. "Although I did not dare to look at his holy face, I fell at his feet and kissed them with many tears in my eyes", Saint Paisius wrote in his autobiography. He begged, "Holy Father, receive me for God's mercy, I will obey to you in everything as I obey to God. If I will not listen to you, beat me and cast me away as you would a mangy dog." He bitterly wept long time. His face swelled because of the abundant tears flowing down it. However, with much compassion, the humble, love-filled hermit asked him not to be discouraged, gave him useful spiritual advice and, fully understanding the youth's real needs in that stage, directed him to a monastic life.

Pyotr went to Moshinsky Monastery and from there to Motreansky Monastery. Eventually he found a place where he could remain: Saint Nicholas' Monastery in Medvedovsky Ostrov (Island of Bears) on Tyasmin River where Father Nicephorus was Abbot. The obedience he was given consisted in helping at the refectory (trapeza), in reading psalms and canons during the service, and in singing in the cliros (choir). In 1741, on August 6, the Feast of the Transfiguration, the hieromonk Nicodimus tonsured him and his cellmate to the rasa. Father Nicodimus chose the name Partenius for Pyotr and Platon for his cellmate. By God's wise will that differs very often from ours, it happened that the monastic community members reversed the new monks' names by mistake and despite all the protests they did not want to correct the mistake. Thus, Pyotr had to comply with bearing the name Platon for many years until he would be ordained hieromonk at Mount Athos and changed the name again.

The new rasophore monk Platon was nineteen years old. He accomplished with fervor all his tasks and did not miss any day and night religious service, undergoing an intense life of prayer. However, to his deep sadness, he could not find a "duchoviniku" (a spiritual tutor, confessor and guide, full of grace, with "a sound and correct understanding, instruction and advice in accordance with the teachings of the Holy Fathers"), and this burning need remained unsatisfied until the end of his life although he strove very much for it (Metrophanes, 1994). The young Platon adapted very well to the local rules. He was doing his podvig of growing virtues, praying and worshiping. He joyfully thought that he would stay at this place until the end of his earthly life. Unfortunately, the King Augustus III of Poland started a campaign of forcing all the Orthodox Christians to join the Eastern Catholics under the leadership of Rome. A representative of the authorities tried to convince the Abbot to obey and because the whole monastic community opposed, the church was closed and the monks dispersed.

Filled with repulsion and bitterness, Platon decided to run anywhere where there was peace and no oppression. Therefore, he returned back to the Russian part of Ukraine over Dnieper River with the firm thought of remaining in his country as long as possible. Only the Lord knew that his stay would not be very long and Platon would change his mind.

He headed to Lavra of Caves in Kyiv (Saint Kyivo-Pecherska Lavra), where a good friend of his father, Timoteus Sherbatzky, was archimandrite. For his monastic obedience Platon was entrusted with engraving brass icons at the typography shop, with singing in the choir and with reading the canons at Church services. As he wrote in his autobiography, the time spent at Lavra brought a very great benefit to his soul. He found at Lavra so much holiness and so many monks he could learn from, that he decided to remain there for the rest of his life.

One day, the widow of his older brother came from Poltava with her own brother and her uncle to venerate the icons in the church. She visited him at his monastic cell. She told him about his mother, Irina, who, because of too much sorrow, refused to eat and after several years became deathly ill. Lying on her deathbed she had a vision which frightened her terribly. "Then as the opening of a book, the world of the Holy Fathers opened the eyes of her heart" (Akathist, Ikos 4, in *The bicentennial of St. Paisius Velichkovsky*, 1994b).

She asked the others to bring quickly the Book of Akathists and without interruption she fevershly read Mother of God's Akathist one day and one night. Eventually she stopped and stayed still, with her eyes looking straight to the ceiling. The people around understood she had another vision. She cried out that she accepted God's will and did not weep for her son anymore. She called a priest for confession and, later, despite her old age, she and her sister entered a monastery near Poltava. According to the biography written by Reader Gregory, they became Nun Juliana and Nun Agapi, respectively. Further, in his autobiography, Saint Paisius mentioned that after ten years spent in that sacred place his mother departed for the eternal life in complete peace.

After one year of staying at Lavra, a God-pleasing older monk, highly respected for his ascetic life, virtues and deep faith and wisdom, called Platon inside his cell and expressed a profound regret that soon Platon will leave for other lands. Platon did not trust this foresight because he had already become highly attached to the place. However, one day his old friend Alexis Filevici from Kyiv, visited the church and looked for him. This person was the very school mate with whom Platon had planned in the past to travel to Moldavia or Ugrovlahia where there was no persecution from the Eastern Catholics. Despite Platon's definitive decision of belonging to Lavra, Alexis insisted on going to the far places where they dreamed so long ago of experiencing complete peace, hesichia, and sinking deep into inner prayer. The immeasurable love Platon had for Alexis made him renounce his previous decision and fired in him a fervent desire to respond to the irresistible call of God voiced through his old friend. They prayed with tears for Lord's help for their planned departure.

After an adventurous journey, walking in knee-deep snow during the night and avoiding all villages in order to prevent any suspicion from the authorities, attacked by two thieves but helped by the men who had agreed to guide them on the trail that crossed the border, they reached Alexis' brother's house on foreign land. Though very hospitable, this brother betrayed their goal and announced Alexis' mother who came in a big rush and forced her son to return to Kyiv.

The monks Theodul and Hieroteus joined Platon further in his journey. They stopped first at Motreanski Monastery in the foreign Polish-Lithuanian-Ukrainian land where they spent many soul-enriching hours, absorbing with insatiable thirst the teachings of the loving hesychast elder Michail who was living in the silent peace of a neighboring skete. This old schema-hieromonk shared with them writings of the Holy Fathers and fed their hungry souls from his deep spiritual wisdom. Platon confided to Elder Michail his secret wishes of going to Walachia. The Elder, who had spent many years as a hermit not only in Russia but also in Moldavia and Walachia (Ugrovlachia) praised Platon's thought and advised him to go all the way East and South to the Saint Nicholas' Treisteny Monastery in Walachia near Focșani, where his beloved disciple, hieromonk Dometius was undergoing his podvig of prayer and worship to the Lord.

Always in prayer and unknowingly protected by God, they traveled without being attacked, robbed or killed to a place downstream from Mohyliv where they crossed Dniester River by boat. Great was the happiness when finally, Platon reached the territory for which he had longed for so many years; this goal was paid with many struggles and much suffering but also with much spiritual learning and useful experience.

Saint Paisius wrote in his autobiography, "When we put our foot on Moldavian land, we felt the great joy that by God's grace we managed to reach this Orthodox country, and freed of any fear we walked joyously praising the Lord." At that time the Romanian territory was full of sketes and monasteries, which as Saint Paisius' biographer Gregory the Reader wrote, "adorned the earth like stars in the sky" (Zamfirescu, 1996). They passed through Orhei, halted at the Condritza Skete belonging to the famous Capriana Monastery, founded in 1429 by the brave Moldavian voivode Stephen the Great (canonized as a Saint in 1992). The hieromonk Nicholas welcomed them and they enjoyed his warm hospitality, getting a good, well-deserved rest. Platon's travel companions, monks Theodul and Ieroteus remained at Capriana. The young Platon continued his journey in the company of Father Anthony, a hieromonk from Capriana. They passed the rivers Prut and Siret, reached Odobesti and crossed the Moldavian border into Walachia where they met Father Michael's disciple, the hieromonk Dometius. It was the year 1745.

THE FIRST PERIOD SPENT ON ROMANIAN LAND. Platon went first to the Romanian Dolgoutsy (Dălgăuți) Skete and then to Treisteny (Trăisteni) Skete, both in the Buzău Mountains. These sketes were under the spiritual leadership of the highly respected Abbot Basil from Poiana Mărului, who lived a very advanced hesychastic life (he was canonized in 2003 by the Holy Synod of the Romanian Orthodox Church as Saint Basil of Poiana Marului). The Elder Basil had come here also from Ukraine, fleeing from the persecutions by the Eastern Catholics, and had chosen this place for its atmosphere of high emulation in practicing the Prayer of the Mind. The Skete at Treisteny numbered twelve brothers and monks and their Elder, hieromonk Dometius, took care that they respected the rules established at Mount Athos.

The young Platon's obedience was in the kitchen. This apprenticeship claimed much dexterity that he did not have and required a long, hard time of learning. The brethren had more than once to improvise what to eat in the refectory because Platon spoiled the food in the kitchen. He never complained or excused himself; this clumsiness strengthened his humility and did not hurt his monastic zeal which increased every day.

He tenaciously did his work of prayers. He did not miss any service and participated with ardor in it. Eventually his inner spiritual labor yielded fruit: his practical skills increased and Platon finished by being much loved by the others. Father Archimandrite Ioanichie Balan wrote that, thirty-four years later, when Saint Paisius was the Abbot of Neamts Monastery, he used to say to his disciples, "Sons, whoever comes to our community should not be discouraged because of his lack of skill in some obediences, for I was also like that. But he should have patience, for with God's help and by his own diligence he will learn to succeed in any task" (Bălan, 1996).

The young monk Platon's cell at the Treisteny Skete was close to a small stream, somewhat remote from the church site. One Sunday morning, he did not hear the semantron calling for the Matins. When he woke up, he hurried to the church but, as soon as he reached the door, he heard the canon already being sung. To his great despair, he realized that he had missed the Gospel reading. Immediately he felt ashamed and became extremely sad. He decided not to enter the church and returned to his cell with his heart heavy with much sorrow. On his way, he fell down to the ground under a tree and wept very bitterly. After the Liturgy, the brethren gathered for lunch in the trapeza room (refectory), and the Abbot Michael noticed that the young Platon was missing. The Abbot asked them to wait and not to eat without Platon and sent a monk to bring him. The monk found Platon weeping and implored him to come for lunch because otherwise they were not allowed to eat. "How could I, brother, go and join the blessed fathers and brethren, when I committed such a great sacrilege, bringing me eternal shame in front of God and all the others?" Platon said. With much difficulty, Father Athanasy convinced the young Platon to come to the dining room. After Platon entered the trapeza, he fell to the ground weeping even more intensely and asking forgiveness from all brethren. Astonished, they looked at him, with shaken hearts for such a sincere, fervent faith. The Abbot raised him from the ground with much love, comforted him, and asked him not to become overwhelmed by sorrow because what had happened was against his will, due to the weakness of the body burdened by fatigue. However, Platon continued to sob and suffer. Eventually, they succeeded in persuading him to eat and praised the Lord that he would come back to normal. But Platon was not able to eat more than two small pieces of bread. After that day, he started to sleep on bench and not in bed, watching all the night so as not to miss the religious services. Seeing his zeal, the Abbot asked the others to follow his example and to pray with more persistence and in deep repentance.

There were many older monks in Saint Nicholas' Skete in Treisteny that Platon had the opportunity to learn from. Many years later, Saint Paisius remembered the gentle schema-monk Proterius of Resetilovka whom he had met at that little Romanian skete. The humble monk Proterius was of Ukrainian origin, like Saint Paisius and Saint Basil. He carved wooden spoons. Full of love, he allowed numerous birds to enter his cell through the window for food. When he went to the church services, the birds gathered in great numbers and accompanied him, flying and chirping, landing for a few instants on his head and shoulders. They waited patiently on the roof of the church until the service was over and then they accompanied him back to the cell (Desartovici et al., 2000). Probably Saint Paisius had this monk in mind besides others when he wrote later about the hermits who lived in good relationship with the wild creatures, "Instead of having a wife and children, they live with the beasts of the earth and the birds of the heavens."

One day the Abbot, the highly respected Elder Basil (Saint Basil of Poiana Marului), visited the skete. He was born in Poltava like Platon and served for a while at the Moshinsky Monastery where schema-hieromonk Michael, whom Platon met as Abbot, was his disciple. Elder Basil saluted the young monk with joy and blessed him. Platon was happy, thanked God and absorbed avidly all Elder's words, feeling thrilled by the sacred peace his presence was spreading around. Saint Basil liked the young Platon and planned to take him to the abbacy to make him priest but the young monk was afraid of priesthood considering it a "yoke." Soon after that visit, the schema-hieromonk Michael came to Treisteny, with his aid and with Alexis, the good friend of Platon, to the delightful surprise of the latter. Thus, by God's marvelous work often so unknowable to humans, Alexis joined his friend, as they had dreamed in the past in the Lavra of the Caves in Kyiv. After a short while, during the lent preceding the Dormition of Theotokos, Alexis was also tonsured a rasofor. His name became Anania. However, they did not stay too long together because Platon with the other monks moved further away at the Skete Kyrkoul

(Carnu) in the Buzau mountains at a two-day walking distance. The skete was in the proximity of the reverend schema-monk Father Onuphrius' residence. This Elder's words of love and wisdom were "most consoling…" From the holy conversations with him, the young Platon went out "inflamed in heart" and "exceedingly zealous for spiritual labor" (see Metrophanes, 1994).

After three years spent in Romanian territory, the rasophore monk Platon desired to leave for Mount Athos despite "the words, the entreaties, the counsels of those holy Fathers Basil, Michael, and Onophrius, who did not wish to be deprived of such a fellow ascetic, because they saw in him the grace of God at work" and due to his meekness, they "called him a young elder." Eventually, "being unable to keep him, they made prayer, blessed him and, entrusting him to God's will, let him go in peace" (Metrophanes, 1994).

THE MOUNT ATHOS PERIOD. The young monk Platon longed very much for the Holy Mountain, the "Garden of Theotokos." He looked his entire life for a spiritual father and a wise, God-loving confessor, for advising and leading him thoroughly in his ardent labor and podvig. He hoped that he would find him at Mount Athos. Consequently, Platon asked for blessing and forgiveness from all the Romanian Skete's brethren, and left for Greece. He was twenty-four years old when he arrived at the Great Lavra Monastery on July 4, 1746, on the eve of Saint Athanasius' Feast Day. There he hit his first obstacle in his striving for enriching his soul with the Lord's blessed grace. Platon and his companion on his journey, hieromonk

Tryphon; had been struck by a terrible illness during their long journey. Four days after the arrival at Lavra, Tryphon reposed in great suffering. By God's will, the young Platon survived and, thanks to the Russian monks who tenderly took care of him, he recovered. He lived then a hermit's life in solitude near the Pantokrator Monastery.

The young brother Platon knew very well the phylocalic teachings of the great ascetic Abba Saint Makarios of Egypt (300-391) who used to say that for a hermit (and eventually for every Christian) the inner war, the podvig, succeeds in taking off the vices one by one like peeling off the skin of an onion. Thus, all his life the hermit removes "anger, envy, fear, anguish, anxiety, hate, lust, slothfulness, avarice, judgmental, overindulgence" and others.

In the innermost chamber dwells the serpent of self-love and self-pity. Unfortunately, this last enemy is not removable but it can "be controlled through *ascesis*, watchfulness, prayer and [the grace of] the Holy Spirit" (see Coniaris, 1998). Platon gradually acquired so much holiness in his heart that the ascetic people around him identified in him "a source of light and an opening towards salvation." The Elder Basil of Poiana Marului came in 1750 to Mount Athos for a short visit. He found Platon and tonsured him to the monastic mantle with the name of Paisius. A couple of months later, Blessed Paisius, now thirty-six years old, had his first disciple – Father Bessarion, arrived at Mount Athos from Walachia. Saint Paisius' work as a spiritual instructor began with the Romanian monks Bessarion, Cesarius, and George and continued there at Mount Athos and later back in Moldavia with many others until the end of his earthly life. He, who was searching himself for a teacher and never found one, was given by the Lord the important task of guiding the others on their spiritual path to salvation!

At the request of his many followers, Blessed Paisius consented to ordination as a priest and confessor. The Romanian Bishop Gregory Roşca, who tonsured him as a priest (hieromonk) in 1758, told one of his spiritual sons, "Blessed be this young man, blessed be the parents who gave birth to him, and blessed be those who will listen and follow him. I felt an indescribable fragrance when I tonsured him and laid my hands on his head at the time we said, 'The Lord's Grace…' Even my hand touching his head became blessed in a way that words cannot express" (Desartovici et al., 2000). Hieromonk Paisius was now thirty-six years old and, as the biographer Gregory the Reader wrote in 1817, he became aware that "the rules of priesthood are close to those of the angels and the priest has to reach and keep himself in a purity similar to theirs; on the other hand, the priests' sins will be judged differently from the regular monks and laypeople's ones" (see Zamfirescu, 1996).

In 1759 Hieromonk Paisius became the head of the Saint Elias's (Elijah) Skete that he had founded under the protection of the Pantocrator Monastery. It was here that Father Paisius copied many patristic manuscripts, and translated them into Slavonic. Two Romanian monks from Transylvania were part of the group under Father Paisius' spiritual leadership: Reader Macarius, who helped Hieromonk Paisius to improve his knowledge of the Greek language and Father George, the future great Abbot of Chernika

(Cernica) and Caldarusani (Căldăruşani) Monasteries in Walachia (canonized as Saint George of Chernika in 2005). These two monks later promoted hesychasm in Walachia in parallel with Father Paisius in Moldavia. The new monastic community gradually increased to more than fifty Russian and Romanian members. More rooms were now needed. Therefore, they moved to the largest place they could find in the Monastery of Simonopetra. However, the taxes imposed by the Turkish authorities soon created insurmountable problems. Even with moving back to the previous location, the smaller Saint Elias Skete, the taxes remained a heavy burden for them. In addition to this, the Ottoman Empire's oppressive interference made life at Mount Athos very difficult. Eventually, Abbot Paisius decided to return to Moldo-Vlachia where he knew he would find the peace and liberty so much needed for an authentic monastic life.

"The Most Holy Patriarch Seraphim and other venerable spiritual fathers of the Holy Mountain sorely grieved over his departure" (Metrophanes, 1994). The Saint Elias Skete remained a strong spiritual place and, after eight years of struggle, counted as "a haven for Russian seekers of sanctity" (Metrophanes, 1994), with shining holy men like the great Elders Basil Lishkin and Ignatius. The latter would have transmitted later the Paisian tradition to Russia, especially to Bishop Ignatius Brianchaninov who was canonized (glorified) as a Saint in 1988 by the Holy Synod of Russia. Under Archimandrite Paisius (deceased in 1871), known also as Paisius the New, the skete became a large monastery sheltering a thousand monks. But Saint Paisius Velichkovsky's inheritance on Mount Athos was not only a home for numerous thirsting souls; it was also "a school" with "copiers, collectors and translators" - a very unusual thing among his contemporaries on the Holy Mountain (Metrophanes, 1994).

According to the biographer Schema-monk Metrophanes, Saint Paisius' impact on Mount Athos involved a third important aspect as well. Saint Paisius was actually the founder of the so-called Kollyvades. This major movement started in the second half of the eighteenth century and tried to restore the traditional patristic practices, with hesychastic elements, despite the Turkish oppresssion. It was opposed to all inappropriate innovations and to all fashionable principles inspired by the Western Church. The name of the Kollyvades came initially from a sarcastic epithet, an insult, connected to the cake of boiled wheat, *Kollyva*, used at the memorial services which were held on Saturdays instead of Sundays. Gradually this name turned into a honorific, much respected name, because the Kollyvades formed eventually a major movement of spiritual regeneration, welcomed by all monastic communities on the Holy Mountain. Among its leaders one can mention Saints Macarios of Corinth, Nicodemus of the Holy Mountain and Athanasios Parios.

BACK IN ROMANIA AT WAR TIME. As already partially mentioned, the Turks took control of the whole of Greece, including Mount Athos, where the monasteries had to pay overwhelming taxes. After seventeen years of podvig on Mount Athos, Saint Paisius decided in 1763 to return to the Romanian provinces, taking with him sixty-four monastic brethren. They traveled on two sailing boats: Saint Paisius with the Slavonic monks in one boat, and Father Bessarion with the Romanian monks on the other. Their intent was to renew the coenobitic life at the sketes in Buzau Mountains where Starets Paisius lived in his youth. The Metropolitan of Walachia Gregory II in Bucharest did not approve their settlement, so they moved to Moldavia. Metropolitan Gabriel Calimakis in Yassy (Iaşi), who despite of his Romanian origin had been Archdeacon at the Ecumenical Patriarchy and then Metropolitan of Tesaloniki in Greece, welcomed them with much love and offered them the Holy Spirit's Monastery at Dragomirna in the zone of Bukovina (the northern part of Moldavia). A document signed in August 1763 by the Metropolitan's brother, Sovereign Prince (Voivode) of Moldavia Gregory Calimakis, supported this decision.

Abbot Paisius restored the church and the cell buildings of the Dragomirna Monastery founded in 1602-1609 by Metropolitan Anastasius Crimca. In 1767 the Empress of Russia Katherine II, donated to this monastery a crystal candelabrum and the large Zaporozhye Bell, of 1.1 tons, which was installed in the bell tower. The community of Dragomirna under the Abbot Paisius grew fast from sixty-four members to three hundred fifty. He instituted the coenobitic rules learned in the monastic life at Mount Athos. The services were celebrated in two languages: Slavonic and Romanian. Father Paisius continued the translations, using the many Greek Patristic manuscripts copied at Pantocrator Monastery on Mount

Athos. He translated mainly in the Slavonic language while his disciple Raphail translated the Philocalic writings in Romanian. Hieromonk Alexis from Walachia visited him at Dragomirna and tonsured Saint Paisius to the Schema-hieromonk level of spirituality. God did not spare them of days of sorrow for at Dragormirna, Bessarion, the very dear friend of the blessed Elder Paisius, "by God allowance, departed unto the Lord" (Metrophanes, 1994). The Elder wept bitterly and kept his memory alive with special services every year until his own repose in 1794.

In fact, it was hard to live during the eighteenth century's last decades in Europe. The world was shaken by violence, invasions, wars, rebellions, and movements of political emancipation. In Russia, Tsarina Catherine II secularized the monasteries' belongings in 1764. Poland was divided among the great powers in 1772. The French Revolution shook the European West in 1789.

It was also a time of much trouble in the part of the world where Moldavia was located. A war between Russians and Turks was going on. The Moldo-Vlachian population and their settlements suffered very much from the battles and pillage the two armies wrought on those territories. Many people ran away from the barren and burned land, and looked for shelter at the monasteries and in the surrounding woods. In the winter Saint Paisius moved the brethren into a half of the Dragomirna Monastery and accommodated in the remaining half the poor refugees, especially the elderly people and the mothers with children (Bălan, 1996). In addition to that, a terrible plague broke out, decimating the local population. In 1775 the Austrian troops invaded Bukovina region where Dragomirna was and imposed the rules of the Austrian-Hungarian Empire. The Turks occupied Neamts county in the late 1780's; they were soon pushed away by the Austrian troops who later were driven out by the Russians, eager for new territories

Saint Paisius and the Dragomirna monastic community decided in 1775 to run away from the Austrian army and to move further south in Moldavia. They established their residence at Secoul (Secu) Monastery founded in 1602 under the sign and protection of Saint John the Baptist. New cells were built. Here they did not have to fear the Austrian, Turk or Russian invaders. It was a remote place, which they needed for their ascetic life devoted to prayer. The monastery was "located in a narrow place, surrounded by mountains as high as the clouds and by dark, impenetrable forests, so that in the winter the sun seldom shines there; there is never any wind, but it is always still; only beside the monastery there flows a small stream, the sound of whose waters may be heard as they splash against the rocks. The access to the monastery was most rocky and difficult" (Metrophanes, 1994).

Despite the fact that the monastery enlarged in the next three years, it remained insufficient for the continuously increasing number of brethren. Consequently, Saint Paisius' monastic community had to look for an even larger space. They moved again on August 14, 1779, with the support of the Sovereign Prince (Voivode) of Moldavia Constantine Moruzi and the blessing of the Moldavian Metropolitan Gabriel, to the beautiful Neamts (Neamț) Monastery. Founded in the fourteenth century, this monastery had grown in time as the "Jerusalem of the Romanian Orthodoxy." Saint Paisius added more cells, including an infirmary and a group of rooms for the "aged, lame, blind, and infirm [monks], having nowhere to lay their head, weeping and lamenting" (Metrophanes, 1994). At that time, under his abbacy, the Monastery of Neamts had one thousand brethren of 23 nationalities.

Father Ambrosius Serebrenikov from Poltava was Archbishop of Slovenia. The Russians delegated him with the task of exarch for Moldo-Vlachia for the years 1788-1792. He visited Neamts for two days in 1790 and, during the Divine Liturgy, raised Father Paisius to the rank of Archimandrite. For a while Abbot Paisius also functioned as the vicar (representative) of the Metropolitan of Moldavia.

It is amazing to see that none of the social events of unrest, destruction, and violence in the world around affected the blooming spiritual life existent in the monasteries of Dragomirna, Secoul, and Neamts. There, remote from worldly turmoil, the monks were performing their ascetic labor, battling in their unseen war with temptations, body weakness, and impure thoughts, and acquiring a silent peace of soul while praying and serving the Lord.

THE APPEARANCE AND THE GIFTS OF SAINT PAISIUS. Father Metrophanes depicted Saint Paisius in the following way: "His face was white and bright like that of an angel of God. His gaze was quiet, his word humble and a stranger to presumption. He attracted all to himself with love, as a magnet attracts iron" (Metrophanes, 1994). The biographer also wrote, "While his innocence and simplicity were childlike, his *nous* [(mind in Greek)] was divine and not childish."

Blessed Paisius was given the capacity of "flaming, tearful prayer." The biographer Metrophanes wrote, "I went once at him at Dragomirna after Vespers. I intended to knock at the door, to talk to the cell-atendant and to ask him if I can visit the Blessed Elder. The door was open, so I said my prayers and entered the room. The Elder was lying on the floor. I bowed and asked, 'Bless, Father' but he did not answer as he usually did. He was silent. I looked at him. His face was like on fire. Surprised, I waited a little bit and said again the prayers but louder. No answer. I wondered so much because I never saw his face like that. By his constitution the face was regularly pale but, as I figured out now, the love of the prayer burning in his heart filled the face with God's grace. I stayed a few minutes and I went out without telling anybody about that. Long time later, talking with him, I saw his face shining for the second time. He was speaking with ineffable love, with a smile irradiating spiritual joy; he was uttering wise words full of grace and dripping peaceful delight in our souls. I was very scared though, looking at him; I talked to him in fear. I did not dare to ask my brethren who were around what did they see and feel, and I did not tell anybody about all these; I worried that the blessed Elder will hear and he will be sad for he was very humble and ran away from any praise like from a very repulsive stench" (see *Cuviosul Paisie de la Neamţ*, 2002). The Moldavian boyar Constantine Caragea also described Saint Paisius in a short text that was translated from Greek into

Romanian and published in 1912 by the great Romanian historian Nicolae Iorga. He wrote, "I saw with my own eyes the virtue become reality, without passion and completely without false humility. He had a sweet face with the skin very white seeming to lack any blood and with a white beard as pure and shining as gold. His dress and bed sheets were outstandingly clean. He talked gently and smoothly, without hiding anything. One could truly see in him a man without a body" (Zamfirescu, 1996). A disciple wrote about Saint Paisius, "He united in himself long-suffering and meekness, and disturbance and anger were not seen in him, except for the transgression of the commandment of God. He rebuked and reproved with meekness, he scolded and instructed with love. He was compassionate and long-suffering, with hope of correction" (see Bălan, 1996).

Gregory the Reader, who became later the Metropolitan Gregory IV of Walachia, wrote in Saint Paisius' biography, which was completed at Neamts in 1817, that at the time Saint Paisius had lived at Sekoul Monastery, he had not been able to walk outside his cell because his body was weakened by long fasting and prayer. Therefore, he spent the whole day in his room as though in a tomb. From morning until noon, he answered the questions and requests of the brethren, and then, locking the door, he stayed undisturbed in his cell from noon until the next morning. Schema-monk Metrophanes wrote, "One can only be astonished at how he wrote, for he was most infirm in body and had wounds on his whole right side. On the bed where he lay, he surrounded himself with books." With "a candle in the middle" he was "sitting bent over like a small child" and "would write the whole night long, forgetting both the infirmity of his body and his severe pains and the labor" (Metrophanes, 1994).

Humility was the major virtue of Saint Paisius. He upbraided himself always and if something wrong happened in the community, he blamed himself and said that his own many sins caused the problem. If by contrary, something good occurred within the monastic members he said that this was due to their prayers. Since his youth he ran away from any praise or glory. This is why, as biographer Metrophanes wrote, Saint Paisius refused to follow his mother's desire of serving at the church altar where his father and grandfather served, being surrounded by important clergy persons, praised, complimented and viewed respectfully by the parishioners (see *Cuviosul Paisie de la Neamț*, 2002). One of the Holy Fathers, Saint Isaac of Syria (known also as Saint Isaac of Nineveh) wrote in his "Ascetic Homilies" that humility is God's garment and that true humility is reached as a divine gift by the Saints who acquired all the other virtues, because humility is the pinnacle of virtues. And Saint Gregory of Sinai, whose writings were part of the Philokalia that Abbot Paisius loved and translated into Slavonic under the name of "Dobrotolubje", emphasized, "There are two kinds of humility, as the Holy Fathers teach: to deem oneself the lowest of all being and to ascribe to God all one's actions. The first is the beginning, the second the end." Saint Paisius walked all the way to the end.

According to the biographer Father Metrophanes, the divine gifts of the Blessed Paisius, were: *a hypostatic wisdom* resulting from a profound comprehension of the mystery of the Holy Trinity; *a godly understanding of the Apostles' texts* which made him a rare spiritual teacher; *a source of important counsel* originating from a solid study of the Holy Fathers' writings; *an unshakable strength of faith and love* despite all frightening temptations proper to a harsh ascetic life; *an unceasing fear of God* leading to a tireless watch for keeping the Lord's commandments; *an unlimited love for Our Lord Jesus*, and *an imperturbable peace, simplicity and humility*. The Lord also conferred upon Saint Paisius the gift of *profound prayer*, which was accomplished with the soul in tears and flames. While deep in prayer, his face was shining with a divine light.

Saint Paisius had the *gift of foreseeing*. He said many times that he saw the voivode Gregory Ghica's head hanging on a hair and indeed after short time the Turkish emperor ordered the beheading of the Moldavian Prince. The Abbot Paisius mourned much the death of that righteous man. Regarding the brethren that he shepherded in the monastery, Saint Paisius carried all of them in his heart and he cared for them very much. The Abbot sighed and wept for a monk in the community, advising him how to improve his spiritual progress. Exasperated by the monk's indolence and stubbornness, the Abbot begged him with urgency to change, saying, "Don't you see, dear brother, the place where you will go very soon?" The monk reposed one week later, unprepared, and the Blessed wept for him bitterly.

Schema-monk Metrophanes commented, "What can we think about these things? Despite the fact that the Blessed Paisius stayed secluded in his cell except the time of Church attendance, he knew by God's grace the status of all the brethren, including those he never met." It happened that one day Metrophanes entered Abbot Paisius' cell when a respected Elder who regularly heard confession from a large number of monks, giving them wise hints with love and discernment, was talking with the Abbot. The latter was reproaching the Elder, "How is it that you don't know what is going on in the heart of the brethren when they daily come to confess to you their struggles, thoughts and feelings? I stay in my room far from them and know this particular thing while you have no idea about it." Humble enough, the Elder answered, "Holy Father, you could not be aware of this thing if the Holy Spirit had not work in your heart revealing it to you" (see *Cuviosul Paisie de la Neamț*, 2002).

The majority of the monks in the monastery under Saint Paisius' spiritual leadership were Romanians but quite a few were Russians, Ukrainians or other nationalities. One day, two sibling Russian monks asked permission from the Abbot to go to their homeland and to bring back with them their old parents who wanted to join the Romanian Monastery. The Abbot Paisius understood their filial love but refused to let them go for two reasons: one, because a monk should not leave the silence of prayer and enter the malicious and deceptive lay world, and two, because they would have problems at the Russian border. The two monks insisted so, in the end, Father Paisius said, "Do whatever you want." However, with tears in his eyes, he asked them for forgiveness because they would not see each other again in this life. The siblings left. They were arrested at the border by the Russian authorities and sent to Siberia. From there they wrote a letter full of regret, mentioning how right the Abbot's foresight was and how impossible for them it would be to get out of prison and return (Metrophanes, 1994).

God accomplished through Abbot Paisius many miraculous healings and deeds. Two people, Panait and Mara from Bălți, came to the Abbot at Neamts with their son Alexander who was extremely tormented by epilepsy. They put the child at the holy man's feet and begged him with tears to do something with him. Saint Paisius comforted them with loving words for their souls, told them to take the boy and leave him in front of the miracle-working icon of Theotokos and asked a priest to go and read prayers above him. Then he encouraged the parents and sent them home, ensuring them that the child would not suffer anymore. Indeed, the boy was completely healed and did not suffer from that terrible illness.

A woman from the rich family Băloșescu was barren. She came to the Neamts Monastery and falling at Saint Paisius' feet asked him to heal her infirmity. He encouraged her with good and wise words for her soul and told her that God will fulfil her wish if her faith in God's mercy is strong. She left and had a dream: Saint Paisius took a flower from the icon of Theotokos and gave it to her ensuring her that Mother of God will help. After a while, she conceived and at the right time she gave birth to a boy. Much good happened through the intercession of the Blessed Abbot as it was recorded in the "Chronology of the Holy Monastery of Neamts" written in 1863 by Archimandrite Andronicus Popovich the Elder (see *The bicentennial of St. Paisius Velichkovsky*, 1994b). However, Saint John Chrysostom was right when he wrote that the pleasers of God are actually respected more for their virtuous deeds than for their miracles (Zaharia, 1985).

REPOSE AND MIRACLES AFTER REPOSE. Saint Paisius knew with certitude when the time of his repose was drawing close; in this sense, the others noticed that he clearly changed his priorities. Thus, he considered that new priests and deacons are needed to continue his monastic work. By God's will, the Bishop of Hushi Benjanim Kostaki, later Metropolitan of Yassy (Iași), was one day struck by the desire to visit Saint Paisius of whom he had heard so many good things. He traveled to Neamts Monastery and for many days he was delighted by listening to the wise words of the Abbot. At the end, the latter asked the Bishop to ordain several monks. After Bishop Benjanim departed back to his diocese, the Abbot said to the other elders, "Behold, brethren, how the merciful God has fulfilled my desire, so that I might see my sons ordained and serving the Divine Liturgy. Thus, behold, myself will soon leave this life." The time Bishop reached the town of Hushi, Saint Paisius "went to the Lord," due to a very "short illness." People were astonished by his clairvoyance, as Andronicus the Elder wrote in his Chronology of the Holy Monastery of Neamts (Zaharia, 1985).

Since the long pilgrimages in Ukraine during his youth, when he had to walk hundred miles, Saint Paisius' feet hurt: his ankle and sole swelled and he had much pain. This illness worsened in time. A Greek traveler, Constantin Caragea (Kostas Karadja), visited Saint Paisius at the Neamts Monastery in 1780. He wrote in his notes that the pious Starets was suffering of podagra (gout) and the stage of his illness was so advanced that the Elder barely could move his limbs (see Diaconu, 2017). Often hereditary, this disease causes gastric disorders and migraines, affects the joints, causing swelling which end in lumps of calcium, and can in the worst scenario lead to heart and kidney failure. No wonder that biographer Metrophanes, describing the great infirmity of Saint Paisius' body, said that the very beloved and respected Elder spent the whole day in his cell like in a tomb. However, the Saint Father carried his heavy cross with peace and no complaints, his great body suffering not preventing him to continue taking care of the monastic community with love and wisdom.

Saint Paisius reposed on November 15, 1794, at an age of seventy-two. During his life he spent 20 years in Ukraine, 18 years at Athos, 34 years on Romanian land and not a single day in Russia. His tomb placed inside the Ascension of the Lord's and Saint George's Church of Neamț Monastery has been venerated without interruption, even during the atheistic communist decades when the monks were persecuted and many monasteries closed. Saint Paisius and Nikolai Gogol are the two geniuses that the Ukrainian country gave to the world.

Here is one of the miraculous events that happened after Saint Paisius' departure from this world. One day, a young monk ran into the Abbot's room, very troubled and confused. The Abbot was an archimandrite, a disciple much loved by Saint Paisius, and he kept with much piety a portrait of his teacher and confessor. The portrait hung on the wall opposite the door. The Abbot looked astonished at the seemingly mad young monk but, before he could say anything, a sudden, powerful draft of air blew from the Saint's portrait and pushed the monk down the stairs. He rolled all the steps down and his body was terribly hurt, bleeding everywhere. The Abbot ran to help him. Standing up, the youth confessed, blurting out emotionally, "Father, I was very angry at you and, prey to an irresistible temptation, I came to stab you. However, as I entered, I saw the icon of Elder Paisius. He looked at me with big menace. The storm-like rising up from his eyes pushed me away and brought me into this sad state. Now, go ahead and punish me as you like." The Archimandrite replied simply, "How should I be upset at somebody, if Saint Paisius protects me with this great kindness?" With tears in his eyes, the young monk asked for forgiveness, and he received that immediately with great clemency.

As already mentioned, the Abbot) Paisius was buried in the crypt of the church of the Neamts Monastery. "The tomb stone, the work of monk Iulian, the brother of the spiritual father Dionisie from the monastery, wrought after the funeral with great talent, was inscribed with a bilingual Slavic and Romanian-Cyrillic text, arranged in two columns and having this content: 'Here lies our blessed father abbot Hieroschemamonk and Archimandrite Paisius, the Ukrainian, who came from Mount Athos in Moldavia with 60 disciples, and many brothers here gathered, and the community life through himself has renewed, and so to the Lord he went, in 1794, November 15, in the days of the faithful Prince Mihail Șuțul, and of His Grace Iacov'" (Diaconu, 2017). He was canonized by the Russian Orthodox Church under the name of Saint Paisius Velichkovsky when Russia commemorated the millennium of Christianity in 1988 and by the Romanian Orthodox Church under the name of Saint Paisius of Neamts in 1992. In Poltava, the Saint Paisius' birth town, a Spiritual and Cultural Center was open next to the Dormition of Theotokos Cathedral in 2008. The Center bears Saint Paisius's name. At the inauguration the Patriarch Filaret of Kijv and Ukraine donated to the Center a much-venerated icon which contained a small box with Saint Paisius' relics inserted in the frame. He said that Saint Paisius' doctrine is important because it shows the way a Christian should live and it teaches us to think permanently of goodness, holiness and purity of heart. Two churches are dedicated to Saint Paisius in Europe: one in Livorno, Italy, and another in Liverpool, United Kingdom.

Abbot Paisius' holy body was exhumed in 1846, 1853, 1861 and 1872, and was still undecayed. The monks of Neamț Monastery continued unceasingly the tradition of having a special service at Vespers, containing stichera, a canon, and prayers for "our blessed Father and Abbot, Schema-Hieromonk and Archimandrite Paisius." They did that even under the atheistic communist regime while they carefully protected his relics and writings from any surprise raids of persecuting authorities. I visited the Monastery several times. One of the visits was not private, for praying and veneration, but within an official guided tour focused on architectural and art objectives. It was in the 1960s. The monk who guided us talked about the history of the place, and about the cultural and esthetic values, but avoided any religious subject. Among other things he showed us the beautifully carved stone that covered Saint Paisius' tomb inside the voievodal church. However, despite the visitors' questions, the monk refused to say anything about Saint Paisius' life, teachings, and personality. The remembrance of the Saint that was kept in secrecy and love by the monks was revealed only after the 1989 fall of communism, when canonization became possible. In 2014 the tombstone was taken out and the sacred relics were set in a shrine for veneration.

One sign of the holiness of some God-pleasers is the fragrance of their un-decomposed corpses or of the remains of their bones. This was the case, for instance, of an unknown saint from the Neamts Monastery. In 1986, a cement slab of the sidewalk connecting the bell tower to the main voivodal church poped out. The Elders decided to dig underneath and, five feet deep, they found a grave with bones that emitted a sweet fragrance. The monks put the relics of this anonymous saint from the fourteenth century into a coffin. Many pilgrims, who come to Neamts today for Saint Paisius Velichkovsky's shrine, venerate also the relics of this unknown saint.

In conclusion, we can venerate Saint Paisius' holy icon with the prayer addressed directly to him in the Canticle VI of the regular service at Neamts Monastery: "Ever struggling, yet preserved by humility, thou didst ascend by the teaching of the Holy Fathers to the heights of prayer; do thou help me, who know not how to struggle or to pray, at least to cover my wretched nakedness with knowledge of my infirmity… As I behold the greatness of the labors and the grace given thee by God, my heart doth fail within me; how can I, having disdained thy commandments, have a part with thee in eternal life? Have pity on me, thy wretched disciple, and entreat the Lord for my salvation" (see Metrophanes, 1994).

1.2. Monastic Contribution of Saint Paisius

THE MONASTIC LIFE ON ROMANIAN LAND. The Moldavian monasteries had a long cultural and religious tradition. The earliest documents mentioning the Neamts Monastery have been written in 1407, but there are many things that attest the presence of a coenobitic community on this place since the twelfth century. Here at Neamts, the faithful people venerated, with deep respect and love, the altar icon of the Holy Mother of God. This wonder-working icon dated from the time of the first Christian emperors and was brought into the Romanian land and at Neamţ in the fifteenth century. It is considered the oldest icon in this part of the world.

The spiritual existence of the Romanian people was marked by a long journey which started in the third and fourth centuries when the first Christian martyrdoms occurred on this land. The Christian faith replaced the ancient, powerful monotheistic belief of Dacians, and lead to a continuous flourishing of the monasticism achieved by a long string of saints, in a harmonious connection with the faithful lay population (Joantă, 1992, and Bălan, 1996). Examples of spiritual communion between hermits and monks, on one side, and laymen, on the other side, are Saint Daniel the

Hermit, the spiritual confessor and adviser of Stephen the Great, Voivode of Moldavia in 1457-1504, and Saint Hierarch Nifon, the spiritual confessor and adviser of Neagoe Basarab, Voivode of Walachia in 1512-1521. These two voivodes (sovereign princes) were canonized as Saints in 1992 and 2008, respectively. Saint Neagoe is the author of the well-known book entitled "The teachings of Neagoe Basarab to his son Theodosius" (See *Învățăturile lui Neagoe Basarab*..., 1996a). The manuscript was contemporary with the well-known "Institutio Principis Cristiani" by Erasmus of Rotterdam (1516) and "Il Principe" by Niccolo Machiavelli (1513). It was copied and translated in Greek, and circulated in several Eastern European countries.

SAINT PAISIUS' MONASTIC CONTRIBUTION. It is not by chance that the young Platon, and later the Hieromonk Paisius, preferred to settle in Moldo-Vlachia (Moldavia and Walachia), and to leave Ukraine and Mount Athos. Hesychasm was introduced in the region starting in the fourteenth century and was practiced consistently in numerous sketes. In addition to that, in the Romanian monasteries the monks were copying frequently from the patristic writings. At the beginning of the sixteenth century, the voivode Neagoe Basarab pled for a virtuous life, knowing very well the writings of the Holy Fathers (Joantă, 1992). At the time of Saint Paisius' activity, the theology in Moldo-Vlachia was stably and unshakably set on the old and authentic apostolic foundation, in contrast with the contemporary Greek and Russian theologies that suffered influences from Catholic and Protestant Churches. However, the sacred life in the Moldavian monasteries was much enriched by the labor of Saint Paisius. He possessed the art of leading. Two powerful communities – those from Neamts (Neamț) and Sekoul (Secu), with several thousands of brethren of Romanian, Russian, Serbian, Bulgarian and Greek nationality, survived him (Joantă, 1992).

The Abbot Paisius combined in a harmonious way specific element of the Romanian hesychasm based on idiorrhythmic hermitage (monks living alone, isolated and independent) with elements of Athonite hesychasm based on cenobitic monasticism (big communities living after rules established for all). He also added to the living system he imposed some elements learned in Ukraine at Petru Movila's Academy or heard from the Russian tradition established by Saint Nil Sorsky (Nilus of Sora). However, he considered that, in principle, the idiorrhythmic style of monastic life is for hypocrites and not for monks.

The Abbot Paisius of Neamts thought, like Saint Basil of Poiana Marului, one of his first teachers, that the ascetic who lives a solitary life labors only for himself and, on contrary, the ascetic who lives in a monastic community works for the Lord and the neighbor, led by an unceasing love for God. The weak believer should keep the royal road of a monastery life, battling together with the other brethren the temptations and passions, among which the biggest enemy is the love of self, i.e., pride. The obedience in the community plays an important role in diminishing selfishness, self-opinion, delusion, and arrogance and increases humility. From the very beginning Abbot Paisius implemented the following rules at his first Moldavian Monastery Dragomirna: "1. monks cannot have any private property; 2. they should be absolutely obedient to the superior; 3. responsible leadership is required of the superior; 4. monks must observe the liturgical schedule; 5. observe the refectory rite; 6. and observe personal piety in the cell, particularly through the mental prayer and the assigned manual work; 7. monks should do assigned chores outside the cell; 8. the superior should watch the level of commitment of monks and even handedly execute punishments; 9. the monastery should have a vice-superior and an administrator; 10. there should be thorough screening of candidates for novitiate; 11. new comers' possessions should be kept in a storage place for return upon possible leaving of the monastery; 12. the monastery should run an infirmary; 13. monks should learn useful manual skills; 14. the monastery should run a hostel outside the monastery; 15. women can be allowed in the monastery only in extreme situations, such as war; 16. a nearby village should have a church with a nonmonastic priest 'so that the monastery would remain free of any embarrassment'; 17. a new superior should be elected only from among the monks of the monastery; 18. the monastery must not be venerated" (see Drozdek, 2014).

Biographer Metrophanes mentioned some important things the Blessed Paisius asked the monks to do: to read the Holy Fathers' writings, to practice the Prayer of Mind and to do prostrations with tears in their eyes, as many as the body weakened by labor and fasting can. The Abbot thought that the confession of thoughts to the

Elders makes the foundation of the monastic life and supports the hope of salvation for all brethren. A frequent confession allows an ascendant evolution of the soul under the careful supervision of the most experienced. Saint Nicholas Cabasilas (1322-1392), the author of the well-known "Commentary on the Divine Liturgy" and "The Life in Christ", observed also that if for the great hermits like Saint Mary of Egypt only one communion at the end of an ascetic life of preparation is needed, for the weaker people the communion should be much more often (see Clément, 1977).

The Abbot Paisius asked the beginners to confess every evening and to have communion once a month; for the schema monks the rule was once a week, for the old and sick – every two or three weeks (see *Cuviosul Paisie de la Neamț*, 2002). "There is no man in this world without sin even if he should be a saint and should live only one day upon the earth," wrote Saint Basil of Poiana Marului, confessor and teacher of Saint Paisius (see *The Bicentennial of St. Paisius Velichkovsky*, 1994b). *"If we say that we have not sinned, we make Him a liar, and His word is not in us"* (*1 John 1:10*). Many of Saint Paisius' disciples took with them their master's teachings into Russia where they founded new monasteries, installing the same rules and practicing the hesichastic prayers as learned.

"As humble and meek" Abbot Paisius was, "he was as strict: for the least kind of unbefitting behavior he gave a strict chastisement" (Metrophanes, 1994). When he saw through the window a novice who walked carelessly and disorderly in the monastery yard, he asked the novice's spiritual Father for a "stern rebuke." He used to say, "A monk must be in everything a monk: his walk meek, his hands on his chest, his eyes toward the ground, the head bent, giving a bow to everyone he meets" (Metrophanes, 1994). The theologian Dumitru Staniloae correctly commented that the Abbot Paisius did not actually introduce the Jesus Prayer practice into Romanian monasticism because this was already a reality for the Romanian hermits, but he incorporated it, with rigorous discipline, within the rules of the big monastic communities (Staniloae, 1979). Saint Paisius also organized at Neamts a school of polyphonic chant, being among the first to transcribe the psaltic neumes into the linear system and to build harmony on three and four voices. He promoted the Romanian language in the religious hymns, diminishing the Greek influence and combining the liturgical Slavonic chanting with the local Romanian music (Telea, 1995).

Saint Paisius was aware that in the community he shepherded, the brethren and monks differed from each other in the spiritual stages they achieved. In a letter to his friend, priest Dmitry in Poltava, sent from Dragomirna in 1767, the Abbot described three precepts of living and praying, according to the Holy Fathers: the precept of "anchorite's peace," the precept of "royal way," and the precept of "community life." He added some comments regarding his experience at Dragomirna. The majority of the members of the monastic settlement were strong. They reached a high level of fear of God and humility, enduring shame, insults, disgrace, and other trials without being distressed in their podvig and responding with love to their neighbors. Others, less numerous, got often trapped in the trials and temptations but they stood up again after fall, in repentance and penance, and they persisted in their prayers. There were very few brethren in the third category; they were weak and helpless, like children who could not chew and eat solid food. They were not ready to take the disgrace and to resist the avalanche of trials. They needed to be fed with the milk of mercy, love and indulgence until they matured in patience and genuine humility due to their prayers with tears always heard and answered with infinite love. Regardless of the fact that not all the brethren reached the same measure of righteousness of faith, all of them strove to watch and follow the Lord's and Holy Fathers' commandments, united by the indestructible connection of God's love on the road to the salvation of their souls. Many years later, at Neamts Monastery, noticing the spiritual progress, the Abbot added a thought to what he had written at Dragomirna: "Our life now is very far from that [I described], as the Old Testament is very far from the New Testament" (see *Cuviosul Paisie de la Neamț*, 2002).

At the patronal feast of Neamts, the Ascension of the Lord, forty days after Pascha, the gates of the monastery were largely open for the visitors who were offered repose and hospitality like Abraham did at the oak of Mamre, "greeting them with love and thanking them for enduring the labors of the road." Saint Paisius had no rest for all four days of the visit and tried to do as much as possible for the spiritual benefit of the guests (Bălan, 1996). Saint Paisius maintained letter contacts with 110 monasteries from several countries, sharing his spiritual knowledge and experience.

THE PHILOKALIC CONTRIBUTION. The main accomplishments of the blessed Paisius were the translation of the Philokalia and his own teachings and writings such as "The Scroll" about the Jesus Prayer and "The Field Flowers" about the dispassion and purification of the soul. The Philokalia is a collection of Holy Fathers' writings which describe how man can purify, enlighten, and perfect himself with the Lord's help. The first version of the Philokalia was printed in 1782 in Greek. It was the result of the work remarkably done by Nicodemus the Hagiorite in cooperation with Macarios of Corinth. The Philokalia is, as the authors said, a book very useful to the soul that is searching for the most proper way of participation in the immaculate mysteries of Christ.

It is interesting that venerable Macarios came at Mount Athos in 1775 and despite the fact that Saint Paisius already had left in 1763, he heard about the latter and admired his work. Nicodimus the Hagiorite visited Macarios in 1775 at Athos where they decided to strive to finish the Philokalia; he even planned to travel to Moldavia to talk with Saint Paisius but due to a terrible sea storm the boat he was on had to stop at Thasos, Nicodimus changed his mind and returned to Athos. From a historical standpoint, one can mention that at the time this important book was issued, about half of its entries already existed in a Romanian version, as the historian Dan Zamfirescu found (Zamfirescu, 1996). The writings of Gregory the Sinaite and Philoteus had been translated in Church's Slavonic language at Suceava during the voivodeship of Alexander the Good (1400-1432). Saint Basil of

Poiana Marului wrote a foreword text to a translation in Romanian made before the year 1749, from Saint Gregory of Sinai's writings. In his foreword, Saint Basil made quotations from several texts, translated into Romanian, from the work of other Holy Fathers as Isihia, Peter Damascene, Calistus, John Climacus, and Doroteus.

It is very likely that the young monk Platon read these writings in the years 1742-1749, when he was under Saint Basil's spiritual guidance at the Sketes in the Buzau Mountains. By reading them, Platon started to practice with zeal what he learned from Saint Gregory the Sinaite's teachings. This probably made him to long to go to Mount Athos. In 1767, the Moldavian monk Raphael gathered 626 pages of texts in Greek, copied from the writings of the Holy Fathers, including those of Saint Symeon the New Theologian. His work actually represents a Romanian edition of Greek Philokalia, issued before that of Nicodemus and Macarios. All these facts lead to the idea that, when Saint Paisius came at Neamts on August 14, 1779, he found a real treasure of manuscripts already existing in the Romanian monasteries which were breathing an atmosphere of very high spirituality.

The monks under the leadership of the Abbot Paisius created a very impressive volume of work at Dragomirna, Secoul, and Neamts Monasteries. They translated, edited, and sorted the texts of the Holy Fathers, and the result of their work was the so-called "Russian Philokalia" (Dobrotolubje) in Slavonic. Saint Paisius also translated into Romanian the Russian Saint Nil Sorsky's written work. Today, among thousands of manuscripts carefully maintained in the Neamts

Monastery, dating from various periods and written in Romanian, in old classic languages such as Greek, Latin, Hebrew, and Slavonic, in modern European languages such as Italian, German, French, Bulgarian, and Polish, and in Oriental languages such as Arabic, Turkish, and Syrian, the avid Christian reader can find two hundred seventy-six manuscripts created under Saint Paisius' leadership (he wrote forty manuscripts with his own hand). Saint Paisius often said that as "the bee collects honey not from one or two flowers only, but from many," the man thirsty for God "who reads the books of the Holy Fathers is instructed by one in faith, by another in silence and prayer, by another in obedience, humility, and patience, and by another in self-reproach and in love for God and neighbor" (see Bălan, 1996).

Dobrotolubje (known as the *Russian Philokalia*) was printed at St. Petersburg in 1793 and it marked a period of intense activity of spreading the Jesus Prayer's rules from the Monastery Optina to all of Russia. The huge impact Dobrotolubje had on the monastic world of Optina is due also to the direct contribution of some of Saint Paisius' disciples like Fiodor Ushakov who entered Optina community. This renowned Hermitage, known as Optina Pustyn, located eighty miles far from Moscow, issued later the very popular book "The Way of a Pilgrim." The book is the story of a man who travels in the Christian world searching for how he can achieve a ceaseless prayer as Saint Paul recommended (*1 Thessalonians 5:17*). He discovers that the basis of such an unusual prayer is the Jesus Prayer. The author, long time anonymous, but eventually identified as the Ukrainian hieromonk

Arseny Troiepolsky (1804–1870), mentions very often Saint Paisius in his book (in fact the authorship is still disputed; Aleksei Pentkovsky considers two authors instead of one - both wandering in search of a key prayer: Archimandrite Mikhail Kozlov wrote the original text under the title *The Seeker of Unceasing Prayer*, and Arsenii Troiepolskii made only some additions. There is a copy of this Russian famous text at Mount Athos. It is possible that the well-known Russian publication made in Kazan on Volga in 1884 under the title *Candid Narratives of a Pilgrim to His Spiritual Father* was based on that copy). Dobrotolubje became one of the favorite books of the great Saint Seraphim of Sarov who acknowledged the benefits of God's blessings to receive the spiritual teachings of Dosophteus of Kiyv, one of Saint Paisius's disciples.

As Moldavia continued to be a center of extreme importance for the European Christianity, parts of the Russian Philokalia were published in the Romanian language after 1807. The last decades of the twentieth century witnessed the publication of another version of the Philokalia. This was the result of the great theologian Dumitru Staniloae's work over several years. This version is in Romanian language. It is much larger than any other versions known until now in the Christian world, regardless the language. This monumental collection of Holy Fathers' philokalic texts consists of twelve volumes.

1.3. Saint Paisius' Teachings

SAINT PAISIUS'S TEACHINGS ABOUT PODVIG. "He who sighs for one hour over his soul is better than one who enjoys the whole world," Saint Paisius wrote in the "Field Flowers" (see *Little Russian Philokalia, vol. IV*, 1994a). He added, "O man! Have you heard of torments? Why do you not tremble and become frightened?" Moreover, in the "Scroll" he wrote, "You will fall, if you do not repent, into both temporal and eternal punishment." These words sound very close to those of the Bible: *"The Lord will judge His people. It is a fearful thing to fall into the hands of the living God" (Hebrews 10:30-31)*. Therefore, man has first of all to choose the narrow path of a real Christian life (*Matthew 7:13-14*). "Live as if you were daily dying," wrote Saint Paisius. He emphasized eight weapons in his book, "Field of Flowers" as faith, non-hypocritical love, fasting, continence, vigil, Prayer of Jesus, humility of heart and wisdom, silence, non-acquisitiveness of things and extreme poverty, and good discernment. He considered discernment being the clearness of mind, while the mind turns its eyes to the soul. Regarding this comment of the Abbot of Neamts, let us remember the words of Our Lord: *"The lamp of the body is the eye. If therefore your eye is good, your whole body will be full of light" (Matthew 6:22)*.

Our enemy is the evil spirit, the deceiver, the prince of this world. Saint Paisius analyzed in "Field Flowers" several aspects regarding the battle with this evil prince. "The enemy likes to hide the truth and to mix the good with the evil. But how can one find out the truth? God's goodwill and all our intentions are meek, full of good hope, and undoubting. Not only in our good deeds, but also in our lawlessness, God endures long with meekness and awaits our repentance. And how can one distinguish the impulse of the enemy? The enemy usually hinders us and turns us away from good. However, if in anything which apparently is good, the mind is disturbed and causes us disturbance, banishes the fear of God, deprives us of calmness, so that without any reason the heart aches and the mind wavers, then know that this is an impulse from the enemy and cut it off" (see *Little Russian Philokalia*, vol. IV, 1994a).

Saint Paisius pointed out three passions that precede every sin: dark forgetfulness, fierce anger, and ignorance [of the truth]. He thought the passions flow from one to another as follows: from insensitivity of soul to the weakness of faith, to self-love, to mercilessness and love of silver, to pride, to love of glory, to love of sensual pleasure, to anger, to blasphemy, to sorrow, and to all the other passions. Therefore, it is always good to take in account the advice found in the patristic writings. However, "if you cannot labor as the Holy Fathers did, begin at least according to your strength. Serve everyone with humility and simplicity of heart. "

The Polish Researcher Adam Drozdek noted the following thoughts from Saint Paisius' writing "Field Flowers": "Faith is the first virtue and faith grows and decreases through the will. Love for God and for people is the second virtue; it embraces and binds all other virtues. Fasting is the third virtue: eating little and getting up from the table still hungry, eating bread and salt and drinking water" (Drozdek, 2014).

TEACHINGS ABOUT PRAYER. Prayer is the solution to all the problems that a person faces in his labor of soul, mind, heart, and body. The Abbot Paisius quoted in his book "The Scroll" dedicated to Jesus Prayer, the words of Saint John of the Ladder. Saint John wrote, "Prayer, in its character, is the communion and union of man with God; and in its effect it is the confirmation of peace, reconciliation with God…, the cleansing of sins, a bridge which leads through temptations, a wall against afflictions." Following the teachings of the Holy Fathers, Saint Paisius recommended, "to perform not with actions of the body and not with the sound of the voice, but with the most fervent will, in all quietness, with contrition of thoughts and inward tears, with pain of soul and the closing of the doors of the mind." In "The Scroll" he quoted the blessed Macarius the Great who wrote, "He who constantly forces himself to endure in prayer is roused by spiritual love to Divine fervor and flaming desire toward God" (see *Little Russian Philokalia*, vol. IV, 1994a).

Prayer requires a certain state of awe, because "you do not pray to a man, but to God Who is everywhere, Who hears before you speak and knows unuttered thoughts." Saint Paisius stressed in the "Field Flowers" that "Prayer is nothing else than a division between the visible and invisible worlds." It is the bridge between the seen person of ours and the unseen Person of God.

Mentioning the Patristic writings, Saint Schema-Monk Basil of Poiana Marului, the spiritual teacher of Saint Paisius, identified the two most important weapons a Christian use in his podvig for dispassion and purification of the soul: the fear of God and the conscience of His continuous presence. The toil of podvig brings fruits if the laborer receives the Lord's help through communication with Him. *"Cast your care upon the Lord, and He will support you; He will never allow the righteous to be moved"* (*Psalm 54/55:23*). Therefore, it is good to live in prayer as much as we can. In "Field Flowers," Saint Paisius wrote, "Solomon, reproaching himself for his excess reasoning, said that it was vain and that blessed is the man who has acquired **the fear of God, humility and love, that is, unceasing prayer**" (see *Little Russian Philokalia*, vol. IV, 1994a).

CONTINUOUS PRAYER. How is it possible to pray ceaselessly? By using a short prayer that can be repeated numerous times and that can respond to a variety of situations. This meaningful kind of repetion is different to the kind Our Lord Jesus refered to, when he spoke to His disciples, *"When you pray, do not use vain repetitions as the heathen do. For they think that they will be heard for their many words"* (*Matthew 6:7*). We need neither "vain repetitions" nor "many words". Saint Paisius quoted Saint Paul: *"I would rather speak five words with my understanding that I may teach others also, than ten thousand words in a tongue"* (*1 Corinthians 14:19*). The Jesus Prayer contains in five words ("Lord Jesus Christ have mercy") or better in twelve ones ("Lord Jesus Christ, Son of God, have mercy on me, the sinner") all the meanings that a prayer can contain.

This prayer is also called the Prayer of Mind or the Prayer of Heart because the mind makes the call for Jesus by descending into the heart. *"I cry out with my whole heart, hear me O Lord"* (*Psalm 118/119:145*). *"As the deer longs for the springs of waters, so my soul longs for You, O God"* (*Psalm 41/42:1*). The soul shows that the kingdom of God is within us (*Luke 17:21*). We call out to God from the depths of our heart with the voice of our mind: *"Out of the depths I have cried to You, O Lord; O Lord, hear my voice"* (*Psalm 129/130:1-2*).

Some people think that calling Jesus' name is useless, but as Saint Paisius pointed out, only in the name of Our Lord we can be saved. Christ welcomes the bearer of this prayer and, as Saint Basil of Poiana Marului wrote, in His love He helps the prayer process. The man who says other prayers looks like a farmer who obtains poor wheat flour by using his little hand grinder operated by his own force. In contrast to this, the man who says the Jesus Prayer looks like the farmer who obtains good wheat flour by the means of a watermill, where he does not need to do anything to move the wheels and grinding stones. "The very sweet name of Jesus and the remembrance of God Who lives entirely in Jesus move the mind into the depth of the prayer" (see Saint Paisius' words quoted in *Sbornik*, 1936).

GUIDANCE FOR PRAYER. Saint Paisius advised his disciples to labor with the Jesus Prayer. He gave them a guide on mental prayer in the six chapters of **The Scroll.** He first called them to a stronger discipline in the practice of the Jesus Prayer and to a deeper understanding of the power of this prayer. The "Divine, ever-memorable and God-created Prayer of Jesus, sacredly performed by the mind in the heart" has been often erroneously said by some in a "babbling" founded "on the sand of vain-wisdom." They risked this way, "by the blindness of their understanding, [that the enemy] might darken this mental sun" (see *Little Russian Philokalia*, vol. IV, 1994a).

The teachings of the Holy Fathers contained in the Philokalia become handy regarding these aspects. As Saint Paisius wrote, it is a great damage to the soul if "anyone dares to undertake this Prayer with self-will, [and] not in accordance with the teachings of the Holy Fathers, without questioning and taking counsel of those who experienced in it... Because Art is called this Divine Prayer by the Holy Fathers, and as art cannot be learnt without a good instructor, getting used to Jesus Prayer is not possible without a good, experienced teacher."

Saint Paisius described, in the fifth chapter of the Scroll, how prayer works. Prayer is a time spent with God, of unification with Him. It is the daughter of tears, the food for the bodiless powers, the source of good deeds, and the forgiveness of sins. It feeds the soul, illumines the mind, and warms the heart. It destroys damaging sorrow and curbs anger. As we can read in the sixth chapter about the place and time of Prayer, if the goal of the Prayer of Mind is the unification with God who is Spirit, the peace of the soul necessary for this unification has to be preceded by acquiring peace in the body. A quiet cell (*Matthew 6:6*), avoidance of any mind's distraction by vain things, pressure of the chin on the chest, slow breath, thought focused toward the heart inside the chest, are recommended. The mind has to be trained not to leave the heart too soon, because at the beginning the mind is bored due to the closeness of the inner space. The mind has to avoid being silent and hollow. It has to work ceaselessly and tirelessly into the Jesus Prayer that will protect it and lift it toward the Lord's love. As Our Lord Jesus Christ taught us (*Luke 18:1*), when we pray, we have to be patient and to not stop due to physical discomfort, mental tension, tempting calls, and need of sleep, because the soul will suffer. Without the labor of the Prayer of the Mind (or Prayer of the Heart as others call it), which is the Jesus Prayer, nobody can escape from the menace of passions and the net of cunning thoughts, which will be the reason of turmoil at the time of death and of the frightening time at the Last Judgment.

DIFFERENT LEVELS OF MENTAL PRAYER. With a rich knowledge of the Holy Fathers' writings, the Abbot Paisius wrote, "Saint Basil, I say, the Great, in explaining the passage of the Divine Scripture, '*I will bless the Lord at all times, His praise shall be always on my lips*' (*Psalm 33/34:1*), excellently teaches concerning the mental lips and mental activities, that is, concerning mental prayer. " He noted that "there are certain mental lips of the inner man by which he is nourished, partaking of the Word of life, which is '*the bread which comes down from heaven*' (*John 6:33*)." This mental prayer, coming from the profoundness of our soul and expressed by the "mental lips," is different in function of the advancement reached in working with it, and of the degree of our soul's ascension toward God.

The Abbot Paisius differentiated in this sense the mental prayer for beginners, "belonging to activity," from that for advanced, "belonging to vision." He quoted Saint Gregory the Sinaite, who said in his 113th Chapter, "Prayer in beginners is like a fire of joy which comes forth from the heart; while in the perfects, it is like an active light giving forth fragrance." However, Saint Paisius understood that for many people it is hard to practice the Prayer of Mind or Heart, especially without a permanent and experienced adviser. Therefore, for the concrete monastic life within big communities, Saint Paisius made the following recommendation in his book, **Field Flowers**: "The Prayer of the heart and mind is for the advanced ones; for the middle ones [the main care] it is singing, that is the usual church chanting; and for beginners, it is obedience and labor" (see *Little Russian Philokalia*, vol. IV, 1994a).

In the conclusion of this book about Saint Paisius and Paisianism, more specifications are given, as the terminology became clearer and confusing notions were eliminated along the centuries due to the contribution of many great ascetic Saints and to a deeper research and understanding on the authors included in the Philokalia. There are three levels of the Jesus Prayer: the vocal Prayer proper to the beginners, the mental Prayer proper to many Elders (the Prayer of the Mind) and the heart Prayer proper to the Saints (the Prayer of the Heart).

2. Treasure of Paisianism.

The **Paisian monastic development** was based on two main elements well-consolidated by Saint Paisius of Neamts: the Prayer of the Mind (*The Jesus Prayer*) and the coenobitic rules for large brotherhoods. Three monks at Saint Elias' Skete, under Pantocrator Monastery at Mount Athos, started on the Romanian territory the important spiritual development called later Paisianism by historians: one monk was from Ukraine (Saint Paisius), one from Transylvania (Saint George), and one from Walachia (Macarius the Reader). Saint Paisius became the Abbot of Dragomirna, Secoul (Secu) and Neamts (Neamț) Monasteries in Moldavia (at the latter, in 1779). Saint George, after leaving Saint Paisius in 1775, became the Abbot of Chernika (Cernica) Monastery in Walachia in 1781 (glorified as a Saint in 2005). The hieromonk Macarius worked under the Metropolitan of Walachia, Gregory II. The Metropolitan of Moldavia of that time, Benjanim Kostaki, was much influenced by Saint Paisius of Neamts.

The Paisian line was exclusively in the monastic environment and can be further traced in four generations of monks. Father Metrophanes of Dragomirna, the author of the most known biography of Saint Paisius, belonged to the second generation, while the great Joseph the Ascetic belonged to the fourth generation. The latter established an important rule for practicing the Jesus Prayer, a rule much respected by the following generations.

2.1. Paisianism in Eastern Europe

2.1.1. Saint Callinicus of Chernika.

This great Romanian Saint lived in the years 1787-1868 and was a direct descendent from the co-creator of the Paisianism, Saint George, the Archimandrite and Abbot of Chernika Monastery (1730-1806). Despite the fact that he was a contemporary of Saints Paisius and George and their disciples, the historians consider Saint Callinicus, who is one of the pillars of Romanian Christianity, as the initiator of the so-called **Post-Paisian monastic movement** which brings specific new elements, extending the shepherding over the clergy and laity of parish churches in parallel with coenobitic communities. Despite the fact that Saint Callinicus was a man of profound and constant prayer, maybe "an embodied prayer", the Post-Paisian movement in Saint Callinicus' case emphasized more the first paisianic aspect: the coenobitic life.

The theologian Dumitru Staniloae identified in the spirituality inherited from Saint Callinicus the teachings from Mount Athos brought in from Moldo-Vlachia by Saints Paisius and George, but also the teachings coming from Mount Sinai (Joantă, 1992). Saint Callinicus strengthened the monastic discipline and rules while being Abbot of Chernika Monastery and, later, Bishop of Valcea. A man of deep prayer and severe ascetic life, he was wise, humble, and full of love for others. Numerous miracles happened during his life and after. He is one of the most beloved Saints of the Romanian people (see *Viaţa şi faptele Sfântului Ierarh Calinic...* 1976).

Saint Callinicus was born on 17th of October 1787 in Bucharest, near the Saint Besarion Church, as the last child of a Christian family. His baptism name was Constantine. The oldest son became a priest and received the tonsure under the monastic name Acacius. After raising all her children to adults, his mother, Floarea Antonescu, entered the nuns' Pasarea Monastery, with the monastic name Philothea.

A rather short boy, with pure face and vivacious eyes, Constantine loved the school but more than that he loved to visit the Chernika Monastery where Saint George, the Mount Athos cell mate of Saint Paisius of Neamts, was still Abbot (also called Starets or Igumen). This monastery had been built in 1608 during the kingship of the Voivode Michael the Brave (in process of canonization) on two islands in the middle of a lake. Its church was dedicated to the Saint Great Hierarch Nicholas and was placed on the second island which was larger.

At the age of 20, Constantine wanted to join the monastic sobor of Chernika Monastery in 1807 at the time of the abbotship of the old Father Timothy, who implemented Saint Paisius' coenobitic rules and followed them closely. The Abbot read with his spirit in the youth's heart and did not ask him many questions, observing how he *"walks blamelessly, and works righteousness, and speaks truth in his heart"* (*Psalm 14/15:2*). Elder Pimen took care of the Brother Constantine as a spiritual tutor and taught him to carve in wood as monastic obedience. Soon the young apprentice distinguished himself with the Marks of Appostleship, *"by purity, by knowledge, by longsuffering, by kindness, by the Holy Spirit, by sincere love"* (*2 Corinthians 6:6*). He was humble and gentle, zealous in fasting and praying, quick in learning the Holy Fathers' teachings. Some monks felt even a little ashamed seeing such a great fervor in this beginner in his monastic duties. In his material obedience he carved beautiful crosses of wood that he gave to the other members of the community.

Elder Pimen decided not to wait any longer for the entire traditional period of three years of monastic testing and went to the Abbot to ask him for the tonsure of Brother Constantine who was only 21 years old. With Father Timothy's blessing, the tonsure was done on November 9, 1808. The young monk Callinicus intensified his fasting to the extreme, and strove to accomplish his duties without sparing any effort despite his limited energies. He slept only three hours a night, not laying in bed but sitting on a small stool in the corner of his cell, trying to *"be diligent to be found by Him in peace, without spot and blameless"* (*2 Peter 3:14*). Full of Lord's grace, he advanced to such a spiritual level of clean mind and peaceful heart that the others came to him for advice and encouragement *"to know wisdom and instruction and to understand words of discernment"* (*Proverbs 1:2*) which help everyone on the way of salvation. Because of these, he was ordained Hierodeacon on December 3, 1808 and remained under the careful supervision of Elder Pimen for nothing leads more to humility which is the top of virtues than obedience.

In 1813 a cholera epidemic killed many monks and caused a crisis of monastery priests. The wise Igumen Timothy decided to ordain the Hierodeacon Callinicus into the holy priesthood, due to his strict life and good example for the sobor, despite his young age. This event took place on February 13, 1813. The Fathers and the other monks in the community appreciated more and more the wisdom of Father Callinicus seeing in him the bright light of the holy Gospels and they asked the permission to have confession at him. The Metropolitan of Walachia Nectarius responded to the Igumen's request and ordained Father Callinicus as Father Confessor on September 20, 1815. Father Callinicus fit so properly to this position of high responsibility that not only the members of the monastery and lay people from the surrounding area were coming to him to confess their sins and to receive both solutions to their problems and God-inspired spiritual hints but also the Metropolitan himself. Father Callinicus found always the most appropriate good words full of Holy Spirit for each of them and succeeded to soothe their annoyances and alleviate their sorrows. Because Father Callinicus was very pious and knew very well the coenobitic rules, the Abbot Timothy gave him also the obedience of Ecclesiarch of the Monastery.

In 1812 Saint Callinicus traveled with his teacher and spiritual father Elder Pimen in Moldavia. After returning back from this educative monastic trip, Elder Pimen left for a time of peace and silence at Mount Athos. Father Callinicus entered under the spiritual guidance of Elder Dorotheus, who became Abbot in 1816 after the repose of Abbot Timothy. Unfortunately, Father Dorotheus was old and fragile. Therefore, he asked many times the young Father Callinicus' help in shepherding the sobor. Eventually, burdened by all the labors and feeling that his life would end soon, Father Dorotheus decided in 1817 to call Elder Pimen to replace him in the monastery. Consequently, he sent Saint Callinicus and the monk Dionysius who knew the Turkish language, to Mount Athos to convince the Elder Pimen to come back. As they were very glad to see each other, Elder Pimen and his former disciple Callinicus spent almost a year together. They visited several monasteries on the Holy Mountain, receiving precious counsels for their souls and observing useful things about the daily monastic life. Later in time the Athonite coenobitic rules proved to be of a tremenduous help to the young hieromonk as an Abbot and a Bishop in his country. Eventually, after celebrating the Feast of the Dormition of Theotokos and with her Holy Blessing, Elder Pimen and Callinicus returned home.

Arriving at Chernika, sharing on his shoulders the responsiblities of the old father Dorotheus, Elder Pimen strengthened the coenobitic rules in the monastery, as he learned and lived on the Holy Mountain. After a short while Father Dorotheus reposed. The next day, on December 14, 1818, the sobor of the Chernika Monastery showed their desire to have the young Saint Callinicus as Igumen instead of Elder Pimen, because they were afraid that they could not follow the severe Athonite rules promoted by the latter. The Elder understood their reason and received this decision with good heart, full of love and ready to provide continuous help.

Despite his young age (31 years old), the new Abbot cultivated respect for the rules with gentleness and loving patience. According to him life in a monastery should be like an earthly heaven covered by the Holy Spirit Himself, "a peaceful haven protected from storms, a place of spiritual joy and healing for those thirsty of salvation, and a place of truth-based knowledge for those who fight the temptations." The Starets should be "the heart of all hearts that search and ask for consolation and guidance, a succor on the way of perfection of God-faithful souls." Like a good parent he combined tenderly care with strictness if necessary. Thus, he sent to other monastic communities the very few brethren whom his God-inspired counsels did not succeed to pull them out of laziness, disobedience and especially slander, "the death of soul."

Saint Callinicus took care in finishing in less than two years the iconographic painting of Saint Nicholas' church on the big island. Appreciating his worthiness and ardor dedicated to the Lord's house, Metropolitan Dionysius Lupu honored him with the rank of Archimandrite. Saint Callinicus supervised several other monasteries as Pasarea, Tiganesti and Caldarusani, sketes as Icoana, Chigiu, Poiana Marului, Ciorogarla, and parish churches in Branesti, Campina, Ghenoaia, and Tohani.

It was not easy to live in those days. In 1821 a revolution for independence broke forth under the leadership of Tudor Vladimirescu and the oppressive Turkish power sent its army into the country. The population from Bucharest looked for refuge and many were offered shelter by Abbot Callinicus who moved the monks into the first island which was more exposed, in order to host the refugees in a place more protected - in the cells surrounding the old Saint Nicholas' Church from the remote second island which was larger. The Turks came and installed cannons around the islands to destroy the monastery. The Abbot and all the brethren and guests spent the whole night in fervent prayers. The next morning, he sent a messenger to the military high-ranked leader (Pasha) who camped in the neighboring village, explaining that no rebels are in the monastery but poor people, old men and women, mothers with children. To the surprise of all, by God's will, the leader countermanded his orders, called off the siege and even sent some soldiers to guard the monastery against villains who used the opportunity of the existent turmoil and disorder to attack and rob the frightened population.

The problem of housing such a large number of refugees was that they also needed food. The monastery quickly finished what they had in stock because naturally there is not much food in an ascetic living environment. Full of compassion for the sheltered population, Saint Callinicus knelt and prayed with tears in front of the icons of Theotokos and Saint Nicholas for long time. Not later than the hour he finished his prayers and stood up, five ox-pulled wagons full of dry pieces of bread came at the gate of the monastery, from the orders of that Pasha camped in the neighboring village.

The region around Bucharest, the capital of the country, was full of Turkish troops. Another Pasha camped in the village Pantelimon and he took a nun for his delight from the neighboring monastery of Pasarea. After the Abbot Callinicus heard that, he moved all the nuns far away to Snagov Monastery and, without any fear, complained to the authorities in Bucharest. Consequently, the Pascha was reprimanded and forced to release the nun. Tormented by an ardent desire for revenge, the Pasha swore he would plunder the Chernika Monastery and kill the Abbot. Saint Callinicus knelt again at the Holy Icons, prayed with tears and called all the brethren to a prayer watch for the whole night. The Pasha ordered a coffee before going in the middle of the night to attack the monastery. The servant who brought the coffee took out a hand gun and shot his master. By God's miraculous will, the bullet stopped in the belly belt full of golden coins, and did not harm the officer. However, this was enough to scare him and to revive his conscience and fear of God. After counseling with his adjuvants, he decided to do something good to the monastery and sent the bag of money he had in his pocket belt to the Abbot to build a fountain. Saint Callinicus did not trust them, suspecting a trap. Therefore, he said to the Turks that if they are honest with their offer, they can dig themselves a fountain at the entrance to the first island. They did and even today the pilgrims can enjoy the good, refreshing water of the so-called "Turk's Fountain."

One holy gift Saint Callinicus had was reading the thoughts of others. Later, in the years he was Bishop at Ramnicu Valcea, he used this in his loving relationship with his disciples. In 1854 his prayers caused the miracle of turning the not-decayed body of a dead wealthy man into dust. He healed a woman possessed by an evil spirit and a boy from epilepsy. After three days of staying at Lainici Skete he walked back to his

Bishop place on mountain trails. Suddenly he halted, sat down and wept. One of the disciples thought the cause was tiredness after severe fasting and long hours of work. The Saint told him gently that the cause was the repose of Elder Nicander, the Abbot of Chernika. Later they checked and indeed at the very hour and day Saint Callinicus wept, the Abbot reposed at the over-150-mile-far monastery. Many were the miracles that happened during the activity of this very beloved holy person but, using the Saint John Chrysostom's words as we already did when we talked about Saint Paisius, the pleasers of God are actually respected more for their virtuous deeds than for their deeds of wonder.

One morning in July 1829, Saint Callinicus prayed quietly the Akathist Hymn of Saint Nicholas while secluded in his cell. Tired from fasting, work and especially the long nightly prayers, he fell asleep at the sixth ikos: "Deliver Father Nicholas with your prayers the people from the siege made by demons, you who with the streams of your sweat extinguished the multitude of the pagan gods, and give us, Holy Hierarch, good healing from our infirmities…" In his dream he had a vision of Saint Nicholas dressed in his bright bishop's vestments accompanied by Saint George in his glorious soldier's armor. Behind them he could see Elder George, who was the cell mate of Saint Paisius at Mount Athos and the much-respected Abbot of Chernika Monastery. All three asked Father Callinicus to build a new church in the small island, where there were only a few little houses. They ensured him of their entire help. Worried that this might have been a trap from the Tempter who likes to deceive the people and lure them into sin and evil, the young

Callinicus went immediately to ask advice from his spiritual teacher, Elder Pimen. Surprisingly, Father Pimen had the same dream three times which means it was truly a divine message.

Saint Great Martyr George kept his promise. After the failure of Tudor Vladimirescu's uprising for independence, several boyars (members of the nobility class) conspired with a political goal in mind. They created a fund to cover the expenses of their plan and kept it with Bishop Ioannicius in Bucharest. The idea was that if they did not succeed and had to escape from Walachia to escape arrest, the money would be used for building a church.

When cholera broke out in Bucharest in 1831, Bishop Ioannicius gave the money to Saint Callinicus who started to build the Saint George's Church of the Chernika Monastery in the small island in 1832. The church was finished in 1838 and consecrated on August 6, on the Great Feast of the Transfiguration of the Lord on Mount Tabor. By God's will, an earthquake tested the solidity of the buiding in 1838. Saint Callinicus restored it and surrounded it with monks' cells and with walls of protection. After Saint Callinicus finished this work in 1842, he built a parish church in Buesti village and a church at Pasarea Monastery of nuns.

Saint Callinicus was beloved by all the Wallachian population who praised his wisdom and holiness. The clergy and monastic world also loved and cherished him. He was elected several times for the Metropolitan position but he refused. All of this made some people jealous and one day the evil struck. Somebody within the Chernika Monastery poisoned him. Saint Callinicus was on the brink of his death to the great sorrow of the sobor. However, God answered his prayers and, in his agony, he heard a voice saying that he would recover and would have to do the necessary shepherding work of Bishop of Ramnicu Valcea, which indeed happened after a very short while.

In 1850 the new Voivode Barbu Stirbei asked for election of new bishops in order to fill the gaps. Thus, under pressure, Saint Callinicus accepted the nomination with reluctance, bid farewell from Chernica where Archimandrite Nikander replaced him, and prepared to leave the monastery where he had lived almost 43 years. The great bell rang, the 350 monks including the sick ones gathered to embrace him with tears in their eyes and to receive their 32-year-long Igumen's parental blessing. After saying the Prayer of Forgiveness, Saint Callinicus reminded them to keep unaltered the good coenobitic rules established for so long. He took with him a few monks to assist him in his new position and left.

On his way to the diocese, people waited for him in towns and villages to greet him joyously with bread and salt which is the traditional symbol of hospitality. In Craiova, the city of the diocese headquarters since 1847, the Saint Demetrius' Church was full of clergy and people to welcome the Bishop. The bells of all churches in the city were ringing as they traditionally do on Easter Day.

Saint Callinicus started his Bishop's activities right away. He travelled through villages and monasteries offering parental care, spiritual counsel, wise correction where needed. He ordained priests and did apostolic work without any rest. He consoled, kindly advised, and healed souls. He was full of mercy and compassion for the suffering. His residence became a material and spiritual shelter for the poor. As war between Russians and Turks ravaged the Wallachian land in 1854 and Turkish troops settled in Craiova where the Bishop's headquarters were, Bishop Callinicus was called back to Bucharest but he decided to continue his shepherding work and went to the former center of the diocese, the small town of Ramnicu Valcea. There he restored the church, the seminary and the other buildings, and repaired the damage caused by the big fire of 1847. Like Saint Paisius of Neamts, he multiplied the sacred writings needed by monasteries and laypeople. However, he did that not by hand copying but by using a printing press he installed in Craiova. He wrote a Lamentation in verses, a book of spiritual advice for monks and a book about the historic events of 1821.

After 17 years of fruitful work as Bishop, Saint Callinicus, now 80 years old, wanted to return to his familiar place, Chernika Monastery, for the short time he felt that was left of his earthly life. He was not so much worn out from the sixty-two years of serving the Lord but from his excessive ascetic labor. Once he arrived at the monastery where he had lived for forty-three years, he prayed for long hours before the holy icons in the churches Saint George and Saint Nicholas. He joyously greeted the very few still-alive monks from the time he was their abbot. He served the Divine Liturgy with them and gave them prosphora after the service. Then he entered his cell as in a tomb, where he would spend almost one year. Two weeks before falling asleep, he told his faithful disciple Alexander

Baldovin that on April 11, he was going to leave this world. He also indicated the vestments he desired for his burial. On the Great and Holy Thursday, he asked the brethren to pray for him because his departure would be soon. Seven priests came that day and gave him Holy Unction. On the day of Holy Resurrection, on April 7, a priest served the Divine Liturgy in his cell and gave him the Holy Communion.

On April 11, 1868, at five o'clock in the morning of Bright Thursday, Saint Callinicus asked his disciple Germanus to help him to change his sweaty shirt with a clean one because "several great people" entered the cell to take him for the final journey. He stood up, walked without any help to the place where he washed his face and combed his hair. Then he blessed all the seen and unseen people present in the cell. He lay back on the bed and soon he asked for a cross. He kissed the Holy Cross and prayed for help from her. After telling his disciples, "I will see you in the happiness of the other world", he leaned his head on Germanus' chest, breathed deeply three times and entered the immobility of his body while his soul departed.

Two days later, Metropolitan of Walachia Niphon came with four Bishops for the funeral service. Saint Callinicus' body was buried in the narthex of the church he had built in the small island: Saint George's Church.

No goods or wealth were found after his repose. He had given everything to widows and orphans, to the poor and the sick, and to fundraisers for building churches, while he was alive. The wealth at the time of his repose was a spiritual one; it was in the hearts of the people he shepherded and especially in the

Kingdom of Heaven, *"where neither moth nor rust destroys and where thieves do not break in and steal"* (*Matthew 6:20*).

Saint Callinicus foresaw not only contemporary events like the repose of Metropolitan Niphon in May 1875 and the Romanian Independence War of 1877 but also later events such as World War I. His predictions were very accurate.

By God's powerful will, he was canonized by the Holy Synod of the Romanian Orthodox Church, under Patriarch Justinian Marina, on October 20, 1955. This was an unbelievable event in a black decade of oppression from the atheistic communist government, a decade marked by the tragic construction attempt of the Danube-Black Sea Canal which was used for exterminating thousands of people in numerous labor camps, and by a giant wave of arrests with the goal of destroying the human being as much as possible, of frightening and enslaving the population. Saint Callinicus was the only saint ever canonized during the 40-year communist era in Romania.

The holy relics have been carefully washed by the Patriarch's own hands, anointed with myrrh and carefully relocated in a new coffin. They were carried the next day, Sunday, October 23, 1955, by a huge procession on a distance of over 8 miles from Saint Pantelimon's Church in Bucharest to Chernika Monastery. The Holy Synod's hierarchs lead by the Patriarch Justinian were followed by metropolitans, bishops and other high hierarchy clerics from Romania and other countries, by three hundred abbots, vicars, archpriests, and priests, by hundreds of monks and nuns, and by a very large multitude of laity. The people working in the fields along the freeway and roads were kneeling when the procession was passing by. Undercover police agents were everywhere: on roofs, in trees, in cars, in the crowd (see Dumitru, 2018). The Saint Calinicus' relics were deposed in Saint George's Church of Chernika Monastery.

The little house where there was the venerated Abbot's cell became a Memorial House where some old belongings of the Holy Father, including his little prayer stool and icons, were displayed. The door of this house was unlocked for visitors only after the revolution in 1989. The tradition says that Saint Callinicus was disturbed during his long hours of prayer by the deafening croaking of frogs, and one day he begged them to become silent. Since then no frog voice can be heard in the back of that little house close to the lake.

Saint Callinicus, pray for us.

2.1.2. The Burning Bush Movement.

The year 1945 marked the beginning of the third great spiritual Jesus-Prayer-based movement in Romania called "The Burning Bush."

Despite the fact that it grew within a monastic environment and it had large and profound spiritual consequences, this movement did not focus on the coenobitic aspect of Paisianism but only on the other important aspect: the Jesus Prayer. As Saint Paisius extended the Jesus Prayer from the isolated hesichastic hermits to the large monastic community, the Burning Bush movement reinvigorated the practice of this prayer and spread it into the laypeople. The idea was that every person could be mystically transfigured in Christ through the uncreated fire of the Burning Bush (Scrima, 2000).

The end of the incommensurable tragedy of the Second World War has not brought the expected relief because it was followed by a dark, oppressive era: Romania together with other five European countries (East Germany, Poland, Czechoslovakia, Hungary, and Bulgaria) went under the Soviet Union's occupation. This period of more than four decades of communism induced a huge change in the life of the people. A demagogic and cunning system of propaganda covered years of human humiliation and fear, depreciation of ethical values, shortage of food and other vital goods, terror, torture, capital execution, prison, and deportation. The Burning Bush Movement's motivation was moral resistance to the communist disaster and disintegration of humanity, and a profound spiritual attempt to counteract the aggressive, destructive atheist pressure of the government on the population.

The Abbot of the Antim Monastery, Hieromonk Basil Vasilachi (1909-2003, reposed on the Feast of Epiphany) gave the best definition to the first aspect of the motivation – the moral resistance: "Bible shows us that God Himself talked to Moses from the Burning Bush Never Consumed in Horeb Desert and saved the biblical people, leading them out of captivity, *'with a strong hand and an upraised arm*' (*Psalm 135/136:12*). We, at the Antim Monastery, hoped also that we will be delivered from the Soviet slavery… For us, the Christians, the Burning Bush has over centuries represented the Mother of God. She is the burning bush in which the Son of God, Jesus Christ, Who is fire, descended and took a human body. Therefore, the Theotokos, with her words of great doxology, said, '*My spirit has rejoiced in God my Savior*' (*Luke 1:47*). "The Hieromonk Sophian Boghiu (1912-2002, reposed on the Feast of Elevation of the Holy Cross), who followed Father Basil in the Abbot position, gave the best definition for the second aspect of the movement's motivation – the spiritual labor: "The core of our meetings was actually the deepening and the living of the Prayer of the Heart... That one who prays unceasingly looks like that bush that was burning without being consumed" (for both quotes see Groza, 2011). "We were overwhelmed with the fear that these waves of evil would transform us all into an anonymous mass without form, without conscience, without responsibility. Where could we flee if not into the depth of our being? Where could we hide if not in the chambers of our soul? And here the miracle happened – man searching for himself met God; he entered into the realm of the Holy Spirit... During prayer, man enters into a Divine rhythm, the rhythm of the Holy Spirit. The crisis of modern man is arrhythmia" (Braga, 1996).

This important movement was initiated at the Antim Monastery in 1945 by Hieromonk Daniel (at that time still a layman under the name of Alexandru Teodorescu, better known as Sandu Tudor which was his name of poet), who remained the catalyst of the group, and Hieromonk Benedict Ghiuș, who became the Father Confessor for all the others. Very soon the movement involved many remarkable Romanian intellectuals and monastic personalities. It functioned openly in the years 1945-1948, with the benediction of the Patriarch Nicodimus until the atheistic communist government forbade it. However, it continued secretly until 1958, when sixteen leading members were arrested and convicted of up to 20 years of political prison, as "enemies of the communist state," despite the fact that the movement was exclusively religious and did not proclaim any political ideas. Almost all the great Romanian elders, confessors and theologians of the twentieth century, some of them being recently depicted and venerated in icons, belonged to or had ties with this important philokalic movement: Fathers CleopaIlie, Sofian Boghiu, Benedict Ghius, Daniel Teodorescu (Sandu Tudor), Bartolomeu Anania, Antonie Plamadeala, Arsenie Papacioc, Dumitru Staniloae, Andrei Scrima, and Roman Braga.

The Antim Monastery in Bucharest was built in 1713-1715 by Saint Antim Ivireanu, Bishop of Walachia. Because the capital of Walachia underwent many hard times, sometimes the monastery functioned only as a simple parish church. However, the place respected and always cultivated a great spiritual and cultural monastic tradition. Spiritual books have been printed here by Saint Antim.

The monastery owns an important collection of manuscripts and now it hosts the great Library of the Holy Synod of the Romanian Orthodox Church. In the hall of this library the members of the Burning Bush Movement held conferences in the years 1945-1948 for the public which was thirsty for religious culture and spiritual living. Since 1950, in a desperate effort to protect the monastery, the Romanian Patriarch Justinian and the Holy Synod made the monastery a bishopal residence and a patriarchal chapel. This saved the buildings used by the few surviving monks from the insane, pharaonic policy of demolition and of new construction done in the years 1970-1989 under the communist dictatorship.

The Antim Monastery was in good connection with Chernika Monastery, especially in the years of communist persecution, when the monasteries and parish churches in Bucharest were much more exposed to damage and persecution. Founded in 1608 on two islands on Chernika Lake, the monastery continued to be an oasis of deep spirituality and outstanding monastic life even under the atheistic communist regime when, in the late '50s, many monasteries were closed and numerous monks, including some from Chernika, were forced to become laity. According to Timothy Ware, the number of monks and nuns in Romania decreased from 8-10 thousand in 1958 to three thousand in 1979 (Ware, 1987).

It was here, at Chernika Monastery, where the Russian Father Ivan Kuligin (1883-1948) came together with the Metropolitan Nicholas of Rostov, in 1943, fleeing from Stalin's dictatorship terror. They were brought in by a Romanian corporal from Bessarabia (the part of Moldavia that was taken by force by the Soviet Union in 1940) who deserted from the abusive Soviet Army and served as a guide and translator. Father John Kuligin, lovingly called John the Stranger by the Romanian Christians, belonged to the spiritual tradition of Optina and Valaam Russian Monasteries. Sandu Tudor met him at Chernika and insistently invited him to Antim's Monastery in Bucharest. Father John started to visit the Bucharest

Monastery in 1945, and his philokalic teachings and personal hesichastic experience helped the flourishing of the important spiritual movement of the Burning Bush. Father John was considered a Saint by the Antim Monastery's monks. Besides the many things he knew about prayer, "he knew the psychology of sin and the technique of dispassion" (Braga, 1966). He brought to the Burning Bush Movement's monks the manuscript of Sbornik, a collection of texts about the Jesus Prayer from the teachings of the Holy Fathers, including Saint Paisius of Neamts and Saint Basil of Poiana Marului (see *Sbornik*, 1936). Father John saved this manuscript from the great library of Valaam Monastery when "the Red Army closed the monastery and killed the monks with axes", destroying everything (Braga, 1996). This manuscript was immediately translated into Romanian and typed in many copies that spread secretly but quickly among monastics and lay people as a "samizdat" manuscript. One decade later I personally received a fifth carbon copy, which was considered a great spiritual treasure, from Stefan Todirascu, one of the Burning Bush's laymembers.

The Russian Father Ivan Kuligin from Optina Monastery, who descended from the spiritual line that started with Fathers Paisius of Neamts and Basil of Poiana Marului, whom he himself mentioned daily in his prayers for the departed. Father Kuligin's "confession of faith" was done while striving "to speak in a prayer state." Father Sophian Boghiu said that the people at Antim were strongly encouraged by Father Kuligin's personal experience concerning the Prayer of Heart, because this powerful prayer that he uttered without ceasing was alive so deep inside him that he actually was breathing it; he prayed even when he slept. Learning from him, Father André Scrima wrote in his commentary that one can also "read the Divine Scripture in a prayer state," and in this case, the confession of faith can be expressed in a true spiritual vigil state (Scrima, 2000).

Metropolitan Nicholas III of Rostov died and was buried in the Chernika Monastery's cemetery. Father John, the Moldavian corporal and the other Russian refugees were arrested at the end of 1947 and sent to the Soviet Union where they were summarily judged, convicted of crime of high treason and condemned to death. However, Father John together with his Moldavian spiritual disciple were deported to Siberia from where, to the great joy of all at Antim, Father John filled with his wise words several postcards that he mailed to professor Alexander Mironescu, one of the laymembers of the Burning Bush movement. "Then silence fell." He died (see Braga, 1996).

THEOTOKOS AND THE BURNING BUSH. "*Out of the depth I have cried to You, O Lord*" (*Psalm 129/130:1*). We pray to God from the very core of our being. Our supreme model is the Mother of God, the Holy Virgin Mary. "She is the type of perfect prayer, as the Kondak 8 from the Acathyst Hymn of Theotokos at the Burning Bush says, 'in her for the first time the heart of God and the heart of man beat and remain beating together'" (Braga, 1996).

She personifies a perfect hesychasm. The Archimandrite Paisius of Neamts reminded us of the words of Saint Gregory Palamas: "She lived in silence in supernatural manner from Her very childhood, and because of this, She alone among all women gave birth without a man to the God-man, the Word." In her deep and peaceful quietness of being, she was the only truly pure place where the Word could become Incarnate. Saint Paisius added, "The Most Holy Virgin Mother of God, remaining in the Holy of Holies, ascended to the very height of Divine vision by means of mental prayer and was enabled to be the spacious dwelling of God the Word, Whom the whole creation cannot contain" (see *Little Russian Philokalia*, vol. IV, 1994a).

This is why the Mother of God is considered the perfection of the inner prayer and the image of her in the holy icon of the Burning Bush Never Consumed is the symbol of the Prayer of the Heart that all the spiritual hard laborers established as their supreme goal. Reaching the high degree of soul purification proper to the very temple where, through the Holy Spirit, Jesus became Incarnate, is the final step of the deification process each Christian is called to carry out. A Theotokion for the Resurrection sung at Vespers sounds as follows: "The shadow of the Law passed when grace came; as the Bush burned, yet was not consumed, so the Virgin gave birth, yet remained a Virgin. Instead of a pillar of flame, the Righteous Sun has risen; instead of Moses, Christ [came for] the Salvation of our souls."

Consequently, the powerful Burning Bush spiritual movement from Antim Monastery focused on the Jesus Prayer (*Lord Jesus Christ, Son of God, have mercy on me, the sinner*), elevated at the stage of the Prayer of the Heart because as Saint Theophane the Recluse (quoted by Belonick, 1998) noticed, "Unceasing prayer is possible only in the heart." The faithful practicing this prayer had a model in the Mother of God, model so beautifully expressed in the Akathist dedicated to her and written by Hieromonk Daniel, one of the recent Romanian Saints. Father André Scrima, another member of the above-mentioned spiritual movement, noticed that Saint Paisius, like Saint Nicodemus the Hagiorite who co-authored with Saint Macarios of Corinth the collection of the Philokalia in 1782, considered the Prayer of the Heart to be a cross with four arms – praise (doxology), thanks, request, and confession of faith.

Two icons were venerated the most by the members of the movement: the Icon of Theotokos at the Burning Bush and the Icon of the Prayer. The first one, which became the symbol of the movement and sits on a special table in a central place in the church of the Monastery, is an icon very rich in meaning. It is the result of a long iconographic evolution, lasting six to eight centuries, from the initial icon of the twelfth to fourteenth centuries depicting the traditional image of Moses and the burning bush as he saw the Angel of God on Mount Horeb (*Exodus 3:2*). As the Angel of the Lord was in the burning bush of Mount Horeb, Christ the Lord is in Theotokos who is a fire of love never contained. "*For our God is a consuming fire*," as Saint Apostle Paul said (*Hebrews, 12:29*). The final variant, very different from the figurative Moses' icon, moves the image of the prophet in a corner, while in the other three corners one can see Jacob's Ladder, Jesse's Tree (the genealogic line of Christ and Theotokos) and Jerusalem's Gate. The Mother of God with the Holy Infant are in the very center of the icon, in the middle of two diamond shapes – one red (suggesting the fire) and one green (suggesting the bush) or blue (suggesting the sky) which combined make an octogonal star. The star is surrounded by angels painted on heart-shaped medallions which together form a large eight-petal rose whose center is Theotokos. This Rose signifies "the universal Possibility of the multiple states of the Being" and the joy of "the multiple states of love" (Cristian, 2016). Evangelists are in four symmetrical corners of the star and missionary angels are in the other four.

A ladder that is the Ladder for the soul's ascent toward the Lord is drawn on the chest of Theotokos. One can see Immanuel (*"God with us" – Matthew 1:23*) waiting at the top of the ladder. Centrally placed on the Theotokos' chest, there is another image of Christ signifying the Angel of Great Silence, needed for the hesychastic state of prayer. Although "Jesus Christ is heavenly fire, the Mother of God who holds Him remained unburned, untouched, but deified by the Sacred Infant. For us who chose the Burning Bush as our Sacred Patron, this is the symbol of the ceaseless prayer… We are united with God's fire, full of power and light, and the more we burn, the more luminous and closer to God we are. This is the second meaning of the Burning Bush," Father Sophian Boghiu, member of the Burning Bush Movement, said (Groza, 2011).

The second icon, less known, depicts the phases of the Jesus Prayer. The Prayer of the Mind, the first step, is represented by the Mother of God with the Infant on her right, forehead to forehead. The Prayer of the Heart, the last step, is represented by an image pretty similar to that in the center of the Icon of the Burning Bush: the Holy Infant is on the left of His Mother. Both bear crowns and are protected by the wall of a fortress. The Prayer of Heart is the kingly prayer, the supreme prayer. The fortress wall suggests the mystery of the very inner prayer, the Prayer of the Heart, protected from any danger of distraction coming from the outside world. As Jesus said, "*But you, when you pray, go into your room, and when you have shut your door, pray to your Father who is in in the secret place; and your Father who sees in seceret will reward you openly*" (*Matthew 6:6*); and also, "*No one comes to the Father except through Me*" (*John 14:6*). In the middle of the icon is the Angel of Great Silence which is Jesus Himself asking for the complete quietness necessary for this very profound and intimate prayer. The result of such a prayer is fire. The icon depicts in its lower left quarter the all-red face of Mother of God, and in its right lower quarter the anachorets, the Holy Fathers, who lived the Jesus Prayer in the terms of Philokalia. It is the inner fire of prayer that changes their faces like the transfiguration light of Our Savior on Mount Tabor (*Matthew 17:2*).

The Acathyst Hymn of Theotokos at the Burning Bush, written by hieromonk Daniel (Sandu Tudor) in 1947, was part of the prayers and worship services done for Mother of God. It is a beautiful, inspiring text, rich in hesychastic meanings. "Who is this, pure and white as the dawn?/ It is the Queen of prayer, and its incarnation,/ Princess Porphyrogeneta and Lady of the Morning,/ Betrothed of the Consoler who transfigures life!/ We run to thee, burning and consumed with longing./Grant us access to the Holy Mount of Tabor,/ Become for us also a shadow and a dew,/ Thou whom divine grace overshadows,/ So that our human nature in its turn/ May be renewed by a rebirth through grace,/ That we, together with all creation,/ May cry to thee, bowing low:/*Rejoice, O Bride, Mother of continual prayer!*/// O Virgin of the age without evening,/ O holy Mother of the Light,/ Hearken unto us, slaves of sin,/ Unworthy offspring of the mire./ Most sweet and good, most holy Virgin,/ The Key of the Lord Jesus Christ,/ Release us from the curse's bolts,/ Open for us the heavenward Way,/ That having received the longed-for revelation,/ The secret of the beloved Bridegroom,/ We also may offer praises to thee,/ Like Moses who, putting off his sandals,/ And turning his face towards the flame/ Of the Bush that burned with grace,/ Cried in the dusk:/ Rejoice, fulgent Flower of an unconsumed bush!/ Rejoice, Christian Dew through which God spouts forth on earth!/ Rejoice, burning Imprint of fire from heaven!/ Rejoice, Tear which melts the interior frost!/ Rejoice, budding Staff of the pilgrim to the heart!/ Rejoice, Freshet brimming in the inner desert!/ Rejoice, glowing Signet set in the soul's depths!/ Rejoice, eighth Day of the kingdom within!/ Rejoice, Tradition of the joy to come!/ Rejoice, Wonder received in a marvelling spirit!/*Rejoice, O Bride, Mother of continual prayer!* (Kondakion 1 and Ikos 1; on internet, translator unknown; for Romanian version see Daniil, 1997).

The author of this beautiful Akathist, the poet Sandu Tudor (1896-1962) who renounced his wealth and entered poor and humble into the Antim Monastery in 1945, at 49 years of age, as the brother monk Agathon, was, as already mentioned, the co-founder of the Burning Bush Movement, together with Hieromonk Benedict Ghius. He wrote the first eight Ikoses and

Kondakions of the "Akathist Hymn of Theotokos at the Burning Bush" in 1947 before being arrested and imprisoned for his faith in 1949-1952. Released in 1952, he became Hieromonk Daniel at the Rarau Skete from where he was again arrested by the communist authorities in 1958. All the time of imprisonment he was tied with chains and continuously tortured. The officers and guardians beat him ferociously. He finished and perfected the Akathist in prison, where the cellmates memorized it, avoiding the severe punishment for everything written and shared.

Here is an episode illustrating the power of Prayer of Heart, of the Jesus Prayer, practiced by the Burning Bush members. The episode was narrated by Father Augustine from the Skete built on the very place where it was the infamous prison in Aiud. It happened in 1961. Tired of torturing the detained Hieromonk Daniel, the chief officer of Aiud prison eventually decided to subject him to an atrocious trial which would terminate his life. He ordered the guards to throw the prisoner in the cell called "Alba" (The White), a cell with open windows, concrete walls and a layer of frozen feces and urine on the cement floor. It was a very cold winter day (- 20°F), and the authorities knew without a doubt that the frost would kill him in two to three days.

The Hieromonk Daniel was closed there with a cellmate, a doctor. As soon as the door was locked and they were left there to freeze, Father Daniel lay himself on the floor with the arms stretched like a cross and asked his companion to lay on him in the same position. They said the Jesus Prayer endlessly. Soon a bright light seemed to fill the air of the room and they lost the sense of time. In the end, when the guardians entered to pick up the corpses, they remained stunned – the two prisoners were alive. They have survived eight days, in bitter cold, without any food and water! (see "Effect of Jesus Prayer", in Groza, 2018). It is in this prison in Aiud where the Hieromonk also finished "writing" the Akathists of Saint John the Evangelist and of Saint Callinicus of Chernika. All the verses of the two Akathists were also memorized by the cellmates and written on paper several years later after being freed from prison.

Father Hieromonk Daniel died of cerebral hemorrhage after being violently beaten on November 17, 1962, around one o'clock in the night, very close to the hour of the revelation he had in the Lord on Mount Athos in 1929 when he was a poet and a journalist. This day is the Day of Saint Gregory Thaumaturgus, the Miracle-Worker, bishop of Neocaesarea (213-270), one day after the Day of Saint Apostle and Evangelist Matthew and two days after the Day of Saint Paisius Velichkovsky of Neamts. Hieromonk Daniel was buried in the Aiud prison's mass grave. The Christian believers hope that, one day, the Lord will reveal in a miraculous way where and which is his shackle-wearing skeleton, as it happened with many other saints' relics. People have already started to paint icons with his image.

The main merits of the very important spiritual and cultural movement "The Burning Bush" are: reviving the hesychastic principles, reemphasizing the Philocalia's teachings (the first four volumes translated and edited by Father Staniloae with the cooperation of Father Arseny Boca were issued at this time), and practicing the Jesus Prayers on a larger scale including the laity (Scrima, 2008). Many church historians consider today that this spiritual movement and its effects in time were the mysterious strong support of the souls of the Romanian population during the four dark decades of atheist communism. The terrible years of torture and extermination in the communist prisons and labor camps produced many saints, whose skulls and bones secrete myrrh of an extraordinary fragrance; they work wonders.

Over eight thousand monks and priests were arrested in the fifth and sixth decade of last century and, despite the barely imaginable regime of terror and affliction they were subjected to, quite a few of them survived at the general amnesty time in 1964. The spirit of the Burning Bush continued to enlighten the activities of the elders after 1964. Books, articles, and teachings about them or from them circulated typed in carbon copies, in samizdat. After 1989 a great spiritual revival took place and the monastic movement flourished with the participation of the faithful lay people.

Foreign witnesses of the Romanian post-war monasticism mentioned that, one frosty winter day, while walking with a local guide in the mountains, a monk was struck by a sweet fragrance filling the air with much abundance. It was coming from the relics of the hermits who lived hidden in the caves of that place. The same source from "Pravoslavny Blagovestnik" in San Francisco, tells of the tortures the Romanian monks suffered in the political prisons for their faith, and of their faces shining with light in moments of prayer. The author ends the article by asking the holy monk-martyrs of Romania to pray to God for all of us (see notes in Metrophanes, 1994).

2.1.3. Saint Seraphim of Sarov

As mentioned above, the Slavonic version of the Philokalia translated by Saint Paisius Velichkovsky of Neamts, the manuscript *Drobotoliubje*, was taken by his disciples in Ukraine and Russia, and it was printed at St. Petersburg in 1793. The book had a huge impact on the monastic world of Optina and later on the Monastery of Valaam. Dobrotolubje became a favorite book of the great Saint Seraphim of Sarov (1759-1833), one of the most beloved saints of Russia (see *Little Russian Philokalia, vol. I,* 1980). This holy man was a true Paisian Saint, mainly for being a hesychastic bearer of the Jesus Prayer, which reached tremendous power in his soul, and for being a devoted reader, promoter and accomplisher of the Philocalic teachings. I think he can be considered part of the **Post-Paisian monastic movement** in the Eastern Europe.

Prochor Moshnin was born as a third child of the Moshnin family in 1759 in Kursk, Russia. His father Isidor, a merchant, and his mother Agathia chose this name in memory of the disciple and companion of Saint John the Evangelist and raised their son as a good Christian. Isidor Ivanovitch Moshnin was also a stonemason and bricklayer and he had to accomplish the building of a two-altar church. Unfortunately, he died at the age of 43 in 1760 before the completion of the project. Prochor was only one year old at the time. His mother Agathia Photievna continued her husband's work, supervising the construction which took a total of twelve years. It happened that one-day Prochor followed his mother and fell from the bell tower window. To the great relief of his mother the 7-year-old boy was unharmed. A man, a fool-in-Christ of fervent faith who witnessed the fall, said that this boy would become a saint.

The Lord decided to test and strengthen the family's faith even more by giving their 10-year-old boy Prochor a very serious illness. The boy saw the Mother of God in his dream; she encouraged him and promised to help his healing. Indeed, a religious procession carrying the Theotokos' Miracle-worker Icon *Korenaya Znamenie of Kursk* had to change their route because of bad weather and passed by their house. Praying and touching the icon with faith and pious veneration caused a rapid regeneration of the boy's health. Prochor worked in the brick factory and his parents' store, but as soon as he learned to read he started in his spare time to absorb avidly the wisdom of the Holy Scripture and to be captivated by the Lives of Saints.

Reaching the age of 18 Prochor told his parents he found out that his call was to live a monastic life. His mother blessed him and gave him a crucifix that he wore around his neck the rest of his life until he fell asleep in the Lord. When he was 19 he went in a pilgrimage to Kyiv where he met the venerable Hermit Dositheus living ascetically in a cave at Kitaevsky Skete, whose spiritual counsels produced a great impact on his heart. Following the advice of that foreseeing God-pleasing person (revealed after repose to be a woman who was later canonized as Saint Dorothea of Kyiv), Prochor entered the Hermitage of

Sarov. This hermitage was known for a severe ascetic life and for the intensive practice of mental Prayer of Jesus, a manner of living tremendously strengthened and revived under the influence of the teachings of Saint Paisius Velichkovky and his blessed disciples. Elder Nazarius of Sarov gave Prochor the Russian Philokalia (Dobrotoliubje) translated and compiled by Saint Paisius. This book became the most used by the young novice (poslushnik). His obedience task was working in the bakery, helping in the carpentry shop, chopping wood, and lighting candles. For three years the monk Seraphim was severely ill of dropsy but his long suffering ended by a miraculous healing after Eucharist and the vision of Mother of God.

In 1786, at the age of 27, Prochor was tonsured as a monk with the name of Seraphim and a few months later he was ordained Hierodeacon. As a devoted soul loved by God, he had several visions of angels and once, at Divine Liturgy on the Great Thursday in front of the Royal Doors, he has a vision of Our Lord Jesus Christ Himself. In 1793 Seraphim was ordained Priest (Hieromonk). In 1794, trusting his profound holiness and wisdom, his spiritual guide Elder Pachomius, at that time still Abbot of the Hermitage, gave him the task to be priest confessor at the nuns' Diveyevo Convent which was under the protection of the Hermitage of Sarov.

Responding to Hieromonk Seraphim's ardent desire to dedicate himself more intensely to God, Father Pachomius consented to bless him for an ascetic life of hermit in the woods of Sarov. Saint Seraphim lived there in solitude in a log cabin for 25 years, except the Sundays when he came to the monastery for the Divine

Liturgy and Holy Communion whose important gap his daily readings of the cycle of religious services could not fulfill. All these years he did not stop saying the hesychast silent Prayer of Heart. This continuous prayer absorbed the Elder so much that he remained still for long lengths of time; focused in prayer he did not hear or see anything around him, as the monks Mark the Silent and Alexander who witnessed him said to others.

During his long podvig period in ardent prayer and fasting, he ate only herbs for three years. Like in Paradise where man was friends with animals and where all creatures lived in peace, Saint Seraphim befriended all the animals of the forest. Father Joseph witnessed how foxes and rabbits, lynxs and bears, were looking for him to feed them and waited patiently at his door until he finished his prayers. A bear loved him very much; it ate bread from his hand and in the same time served him and brought him honey. Saint Seraphim worked tirelessly around the cabin; he gathered moss for fertilizing his garden, grew plants, built up a beehive, and consolidated the banks of the river. The relentless mosquito and gnat swarms did not bother him; on the opposite, they strengthened him in his interior podvig because he said, "the passions can be destroyed only through suffering and afflictions."

One day, in 1804, while chopping fire wood, he was attacked by thieves who ferociously beat him nearly to death with the handle of his own axe, in order to rob him. He was taken almost dead to the monastery, where on his sick bed he had a vision of the Mother of God and the Apostles Peter and John. He got well but afterwards his back remained bent and he used a staff for walking. Despite his hunched body, at the trial Saint Seraphim begged the judge for a complete mercy for the thieves. Back in the forest desert, Saint Seraphim subjected himself to another endeavor to control his body and liberate his soul: he spent a thousand days and nights on a rock outside his cabin, where frequently he knelt with fervor in a firm, fiery prayer, like a truly Jesus Prayer, with his arms raised to the sky: "O God, be merciful on me a sinner." This super-human effort is extraordinary due to the atrocious pain from all his wounds that had not completely healed. One of the icons depicting Saint Seraphim that people venerate today is showing him in prayer on a rock. He humbly said to a brother who was astonished seeing his labors that what he did was much less than Saint Simeon the Stylite's labor who lived forty-seven years on a pillar.

Like all the holy hermits living in the desert, including Saint Anthony the Great, Saint Seraphim underwent long battles with demons, battles which at this high level of spirituality became material; thus he bore real marks of being beaten by them. Since his last spiritual teacher Abbot Isaiah reposed into the Lord in 1807, Saint Seraphim secluded himself for three years in a total solitude and absolute silence. At the request of the elders, Saint Seraphim changed his forest seclusion place for a monastery cell seclusion in 1810. As an effect of a Divine revelation, after five years of monastic isolation he allowed people to enter his cell, and after other five years he broke his silence and talked with people, welcoming them with the salute "Christ is risen." The Mother of God asked him to return to his forest cabin and to receive there the numerous pilgrims thirsty for his blessings, words and prayers. There he spent his last eight years of earthly life. He performed miraculous healings and helped people with his gift of foresight.

In 1831 Saint Seraphim healed Motovilov, a man who could no longer walk and was brought and laid down at the feet of the Saint. Nicholas Alexandrovich Motovilov had suffered of a complex of rheumatic diseases, with a weakened body, contorted legs, swollen knees, for three years; no treatment had helped. Saint Seraphim checked his faith by asking him multiple questions. Soon Motovilov who was held by the arms of his relatives and of the Elder all of a sudden stood up and walked. Since that day Motovilov became his disciple.

Saint Seraphim reposed on January 2, 1833, at 2 a.m., while kneeling and praying at the icon of the Mother of God, icon known as "Tender Feelings" or "Tenderness Icon" (this icon that also bear the name *Umilenie* or *Joy of All Joys* is now in the chapel of the Patriarch of Moscow). He was 74 years old. That very day people in two different remote places knew that he fell asleep in Sarov: Abbot Philaret at Glinsky Monastery near Kursk who saw a bright light at 2 o'clock in the morning and Archbishop Antony who served a Pannikhida (memorial service) for him later in the morning at the Cathedral in Voronezh. Both locations were hundreds of miles away from Sarov.

The Holy Synod of Russia canonized Elder Seraphim in 1903, when his relics were transferred at the Church of Saints Zosima and Sabbatius in Sarov; the Tzar Nicholas II and his family attended these festivities. A church was erected on the place of his cabin in the woods and another one at the Diveyevo Convent of nuns. During the communist persecution that started after the 1917 Revolution, the authorities desecrated and ruined many relics of Saints. By God's mysterious will Saint Seraphim's relics were not destroyed. The Church recovered them in 1991 when somebody discovered the hiding place in a Soviet anti-religious museum. The relics were brought back from Moscow to Diveyevo Convent by a procession of numerous pious people who walked the whole distance of 450 miles. Before falling asleep in the Lord, Saint Seraphim gave a candle to the nuns of Diveyevo Convent telling them that his remains would be returned with it to the Convent. The Soviet atheist authorities closed the Convent in 1927 but the nuns transmitted that candle from one to the other. Mother Margarita (1899-1997) was the last survivor of the old Convent and she had the candle at the time of recovery; thus, she could light it next to the relics while they were carried to Diveyevo (see *Little Russian Philokalia, vol. I, 1980*).

THE SPIRITUAL INHERITANCE FROM SAINT SERAPHIM OF SAROV. A victorious fighter against evil and its temptations storming over the human soul, Saint Seraphim left some pearls of wisdom that we, Christians, keep in our heart. He warned us that "the evil is like a lion, hiding in ambush (see *Psalm 9/9,10:30* and *1 Peter 5:8*). He secretly sets out nets of unclean and unholy thoughts. So, it is necessary to break them off as soon as we notice them, by means of pious reflection and prayer." But he encouraged us saying, "Where there is God, there is no evil. Everything coming from God is peaceful, healthy and leads a person to the judgment of his own imperfections and humility." Feeling the protective presence of the Lord brings peace in this battle: "When a person accepts anything Godly, then he rejoices in his heart, but when he has accepted anything evil, then he becomes tormented."

This continuous battle has a supreme goal – the liberation of the spirit from the slavery the passions of the body bring, because ideally it should be the opposite: "The body is a slave, the soul a sovereign, and therefore it is due to Divine mercy when the body is worn out by illness: for thereby the passions are weakened, and a man comes to himself; indeed, bodily illness itself is sometimes caused by the passions." We have to learn to separate us from the superficial preferences of the world around us: "Excessive care about worldly matters is characteristic of an unbelieving and fainthearted person, and woe to us, if, in taking care of ourselves, we do not use as our foundation our faith in God, who cares for us! If we do not attribute visible blessings to Him, which we use in this life, then how can we expect those blessings from Him which are promised in the future? We will not be of such little faith. By the words of our Savior, it is better first to seek the Kingdom of God, for the rest shall be added unto us (see *Matthew 6:33*)."

We have to learn to be with ourselves under the loving eye of God, to be accustomed to the deep inner side of our being. Saint Seraphim told his disciple Motovilov, "It is necessary that the Holy Spirit enter our heart. Everything good that we do, that we do for

Christ, is given to us by the Holy Spirit, but prayer most of all, which is always available to us." We achieve this by prayer and by reading the Word of God and feeding our mind and heart with It. "The reading of the Word of God should be performed in solitude, in order that the whole mind of the reader might be plunged into the truths of the Holy Scripture, and that from this he might receive warmth, which in solitude produces tears; from these a man is wholly warmed and is filled with spiritual gifts, which rejoice the mind and heart more than any word." This will help us to achieve the power of prayer, which is like a burning bush because "God is a fire that warms and kindles the heart and inward parts. Hence, if we feel in our hearts the cold which comes from evil—for the evil is cold—let us call on the Lord. He will come to warm our hearts with perfect love, not only for Him but also for our neighbor, and the cold of him who hates the good will flee before the heat of His countenance." The love of neighbor is our visible measure of our deification work (see *Some sayings of Saint Seraphim of Sarov*, 2011).

The supreme goal of every Christian should be the acquisition of the Holy Spirit which is a Divine gift for the terrain well prepared by the labor for deification through a good podvig, strong faith and solid virtues. Saint Seraphim said, "Acquire a peaceful spirit, and around you thousands will be saved." He also said, "The grace of the All-Holy Spirit of God appears in an ineffable light to all to whom God reveals its action." (see *Some sayings of Saint Seraphim of Sarov*, 2011).

Motovilov asked his master how we can know that we are in the grace of the Holy Spirit. Saint Seraphim who already told his disciple about the great light that surrounded Christ on Mount Tabor and blinded by its power the eyes of Peter, John and Jacob, gave Motovilov the chance to experience seeing such a transfigurative light. Here is what he wrote in his memoirs about this conversation: "I glanced at his face and there came over me an even greater reverent awe. Imagine in the center of the sun, in the dazzling light of its midday rays, the face of a man talking to you. You see the movement of his lips and the changing expression of his eyes, you hear his voice… yet you do not see his hands, you do not even see your self or his figure, but only a blinding light spreading far around for several yards and illumining with its glaring sheen…" Asked how he feels, Motovilov said, "I feel such calmness and peace in my soul that no words can express it" (see *Little Russian Philokalia, vol. I,* 1980).

Regarding this extraordinary event witnessed by Motovilov on the great Saint Seraphim of Sarov, let us remember the transfiguring light that the Icon of Prayer from Antim Monastery shows on Theotokos' face. Father Calciu witnessed a peaceful, sweet variant of the Taboric light on Father Benedict Ghius' body at Chernika Monastery (see Calciu, 1997 and Groza, 2018).

"Thou didst love Christ from thy youth, O blessed one, / and longing to work for Him alone thou didst struggle in the wilderness with constant prayer and labor. / With penitent heart and great love for Christ thou wast favored by the Mother of God. / Wherefore we cry to thee:/ Save us by thy prayers, O Seraphim our righteous Father" (Troparion).

2.1.4. The Elders of Optina

The well-known and beloved Monastery of Optina (Optina Pustyn) is located in a beautiful pine forest next to the small Zhizdra River and not very far from town of Kozelsk, in Kaluga district, south-west of Moscow. Founded in the sixteenth century, the monastery deteriorated considerably after the secularization reforms of Russian Tzarina Catherine II the Great. A new and flourishing life started towards the end of the eighteenth century, based on the coenobitic tradition of Saint Paisius Velichkovsky, at the initiative of Metropolitan Platon of Moscow who helped Abbot Abraham of Pechnocha to restore the buildings and community. In 1821 Bishop Philaret of Kaluga decided before becoming Metropolitan of Kyiv to add the small Skete of Saint John Baptist the Forerunner to the big Monastery of Optina, a hermitage to serve as a reclused center exclusively for the Russian Starets (Elders) who wanted to focus exclusively on a hesychastic life of prayer in the spiritual lineage of Saint Paisius.

As Hieromonk Macarios of Simonos Petra Monastery at Mount Athos wrote in his Synaxarion (see it on the website of the Holy Monastery of Saint Paisius, a monastery of nuns in Safford, Arizona), the new staretsdom (Eldership or "Startchetsvo" in Russian) "was constituted as a real antechamber of Heaven where the strict observance, humility and simplicity of the monks were plainly evident." A biographer, quoted in Synaxarion, wrote about Elder Macarius Ivanov, one of the Elders living there, that "his gaze was peaceable, his speech humble and unpretentious. But his spirit was ever united to God by ceaseless inner prayer, in virtue of which his face shone with spiritual joy and radiated love of neighbor." The Elder's lips moved continuously in the Jesus Prayer like a natural breath even in his very few hours of sleep, while in time of insomnia he deepened himself in meditation on divine matters or in chanting psalms and hymns. By the Lord's blessing an uncreated light sometimes covered Elder Macarius' body with its transfiguring fire. The biographer wrote that "his countenance, like that of an angel of God, was burning and full of light." The case of Elder Macarius was not unique because other Elders from this staretsdom were as remarkable. Today the Russian Orthodox Church venerates fourteen great Elders who strived for a holy life in this place in the period of 1821-1924. They were glorified in year 2000 and are celebrated on the Feast of Synaxis of Optina Elders on October 10/23 (according to the Julian/Gregorian calendar).

In exchange for their recluse life in intense and continuous prayer, for their devoted worship, ardent podvig and harsh ascesis, the Lord enriched the Elders at the Skete of the Forerunner with tremendous power of spirit, deep knowledge of the human mind and heart, and miraculous gifts. Saint Seraphim of Sarov, at the end of his life of fervent striving and stunning endurance for receiving the Lord in a pure body and spirit as in a sacred temple, opened himself up to the people to counsel their souls thirsty for God and to help them out of their troubles, confusion, suffering, and diseases. In a similar way, the Elders of Optina Skete opened up themselves to the people in need, helping them through the acting force of the Elders' prayers and wisdom. Learning all the hidden inner corners of their own humanity during their spiritual struggle, the Elders acquired precious experience which enabled them to understand their visitors' various difficult problems. If this small but great center of holiness did not develop much the coenobitic aspect of Paisianism (with a few exceptions as when they guided some convents), it pushed very far for the aspect of the Jesus Prayer and it added the singularity of a wide contact with the needful souls of the outside laity. The Skete became "a lodestone or a magnet to the spiritual men" who traveled to Kozelsk, the town which was in the neighborhood of the Skete in Kaluga District. People of all social classes and occupations, wealthy or poor, village or town habitants, schooled or illiterate, peasants or writers and artists, crowded into the hermitage for receiving counsel, encouragement, advice, or a God-inspired simple word able to bring light and peace in their lives. The Elders could "hear" the discrete, intimate whisper of their visitors' souls and succeeded in building a heart-to-heart and mind-to-mind dialogue that yielded peace, repentance and spiritual strength.

Soon the Skete proved to be so fruitful in its missionary work that its message of faith, hope and love spread quickly throughout Russia. This impact induced much jealousy among other monasteries. They found all kinds of reasons to indict the Starets. For instance, some brethren were scandalized that Elder Ambrose Grenkov spent long time with a woman about a trivial subject like feeding turkeys. In his wisdom Saint Ambrose had realized that the woman's entire life was around the turkeys she worried over. Therefore, his reply to his accusers was simple: "The peace of her soul is of no less account than that of those who come to me with questions about sublime matters." The Elders' influence on laity angered bishops. Bishop Nicholas of Kaluga persecuted the Elders, moving some of them to other monasteries and sketes.

The first two Elders who settled at Optina Staretsdom were the brethren Moses and Anthony Putilof, hermits from the Roslav woods near Smolensk, disciples of Paisian Fathers. Elder Anthony used to say, "Pray fervently to the Lord God and your cold heart will be warmed by His sweetest Name, for our God is Fire. Calling upon His name destroys impure thoughts and also warms our hearts to fullfil His commandments." Elder Leonid Nagolkin was ordained Hieromonk at Belye Berega (White Bluff) Hermitage where he met Elder Theodore, who shared his hesychastic experience gained under the Abbot Saint Paisius at the Romanian Monastery of Neamts. Together with him and Father Cleopa, also from Neamts, Hieroschema-monk Leonid lived in the forest before settling at a skete belonging to the well-known Valaam Monastery. Their spiritual load attracted the monks who were searching for counsel and guidance. The Abbot of Valaam Monastery disliked that, called them "innovators" and asked them to leave.

After staying at the Monastery of Saint Alexander of Svir, Father Leonid joined the Startchetsvo at Optina. However, as with his predecessors and successors, here he ran into the same jealous opposition from the large Optina Monastery, and only by the intervention of Metropolitans Philaret of Kyiv and Philaret of Moscow and by the support of Saint Ignatius Brianchaninov, was Elder Leonid was not exiled at Solovki in the Far Frozen North. Elder Macarius Ivanov's body was fragile but he followed a very severe daily program: he woke up at 2 o'clock in the morning, prayed for a couple of hours, then wrote and worked in the garden, heard confession, worshipped, and prayed.

At the insistent suggestion of the philosopher Ivan Kireyevsky, a Slavophile spiritual apprentice, Elder Macarius started to copy, translate and revise Patristic writings, like Saint Paisius Velichkovsky in Moldavia. The series of writings started in 1846 with the life and teachings of Saint Paisius and continued with those of Saints John Climacus, Symeon the New Theologian, Isaac the Syrian, Maximus the Confessor, Nilus of Sora, Dorotheus of Gaza and others. For most of the texts, Elder Macarius edited in Russian the Slavonic versions that Saint Paisius and his disciples had made at Neamts. As a result, an important library was created at Optina. The brethren Ivan and Pyotr Kireyevsky played an important role in collecting books and manuscripts for it; these two men are buried in the monastery's precincts.

The Elder Macarius's publications spread fast in the whole Russia, gaining tremendous popularity. They were well received also by the Russian intellectual elite and this is partially why great personalities like Nicholas Gogol, Vladimir Soloviev, Constantine Leontiev, Fyodor Dostoyevsky and Leo Tolstoy visited the Startchetsvo and wrote to the Elders in order to absorb their wisdom and to have an inspiring exchange of thoughts with them. Five large volumes of Father Macarius' correspondence remained in the library after his blessed repose in the Lord.

All these facts increased the renown of Optina Monastery and its Startchetsvo, creating even more opposition from other monasteries and leading to more persecution from bishops. Naturally, some of the adversaries' reasons might have contained a grain of truth as for instance the danger of spreading the knowledge of the Jesus Prayer among the unprepared laypeople who might fall prey to spiritual delusions by practicing it. The Holy Phylokalic Fathers emphasized the truth that a proper living of the Jesus Prayer must be done under the careful guidance of an experienced Elder. Certainly, the Starets knew all these things and used great discernment, but the adversaries exaggerated the proportions in order to build up an apparently justifiable accusation. Fortunately, Metropolitan Philaret Drozdov of Moscow (1782-1867, in this position for 46 years, canonized as Saint in 1994) always defended the Optina Elders.

Elder Macarius had a reliable younger cooperator in monk Ambrose Grenkov, who was very proficient in ancient languages. This monk gradually became, in his thirty years at Optina, the brightest local Elder, elevating Optina's fame and its fruitful and influential spiritual activities to its highest peak. People considered him a Saint and a prophet. However, when he was young, he never thought that he would wear monastic clothes. The son of a village priest, Elder Ambrose loved books and was a brilliant student. Unfortunately, a severe illness hit him hard. He desperately prayed for healing and promised, if he recovered, to devote his entire life to God in a monastic community. His prayer was answered - he became completely healthy again. Because he enjoyed the world too much, he planned to do something else than what he promised. To his great annoyance, his conscience tormented him tirelessly. He even seemed to hear the Lord's voice in the murmur of the streams calling him to a hermit life. Thus, at the end of four years of hesitation he decided to enter Optina Monastery, as a local anchorite had suggested.

At Optina, monk Ambrose worked under the spiritual direction of Father Macarius, achieving a solid knowledge of the Holy Fathers' teachings and a profound living of the prayer of the heart. For his journey towards spiritual perfection, God in His infinite wisdom subjected monk Ambrose to a severe trial that would last until the end of his earthly life: a debilitating illness which tied him frequently to his bed. As we read in the Synaxarion written by Hieromonk Macarios of Simonos Petra Monastery at Mount Athos, the illness gave Elder Ambrose "the opportunity of greater self-knowledge through retiring within himself and discovering, within the depths of his heart, the mysteries of human nature and the means of reconciling men with God." This was also the experience of Saint Apostle Paul who begged the Lord to take out the thorn planted in his flesh; the Lord answered to his request of ease with the following words: "*My grace is sufficient for you, for My strength is made perfect in weakness*" (*2 Corinthians 12: 9*).

Elder Macarius suggested that all the other Starets to go to Elder Ambrose for confession. Soon laypeople also started to crowd the entrance at his cell. Even though frequently bedridden, Saint Ambrose received visitors every day, from 9 a.m. to 11 p.m., and listened with gentle and unwearied patience to their problems.

During the rest of the time he answered about forty letters daily. His deep-penetrating insight springing from continuous prayer reached the most obscure corners of people's consciences, and only two or three words sufficed in solving their dilemmas, consoling them in trouble, and redirecting them to the right way of virtue and repentance. Being permanently present in the intimate dialogue held by the Elder's unceasing inner prayer, God was speaking to the people through His beloved servant. "*Do not worry about how or what you should speak. For it will be given to you in that hour what you should speak; for it is not you who speak, but the Spirit of your Father who speaks in you*" (*Matthew 10:19-20*). Saint Ambrose had the right words for everyone, from the upper spheres of high-level philosophy to the down-to-earth aspects of daily life. His sayings were providential and changed the lives of many people who sought his advice.

The intellectuals found in him an ideal interlocutor for their theoretical subjects. Vasily Zhukovsky, the brethren Ivan and Konstantin Aksakov, Pyotr Tchaikovsky, Nikolai Gogol, Ivan Turgenev, Vladimir Solovyov and Vasily Rozanov liked to come to Optina. Full of unanswered questions, the philosopher Konstantin Leontyev decided to settle at the monastery for four years; at the end of this period he wanted to enter the monastic life and he was tonsured. A certain writer discovered "an unfathomable abyss of charity" in the Elder Ambrose.

Deeply depressed after losing his son Alyosha, the great writer Fyodor Dostoyevsky found comfort in Father Ambrose's love filled words and returned home transformed, with a reinvigorated heart. Consequently, he modified the novel he was working on, and introduced two new characters: a youth with purity of heart bearing the name of the writer's deceased son and an ideal Elder bearing the name Zosima based on Father Ambrose's features. The resultant novel is his famous masterpiece *The Brothers Karamazov*. The other pinnacle of Russian literature, Leo Tolstoy, also found satisfaction from his visits to the Elder Ambrose. In the proximity of the latter Tolstoy felt "the nearness of God" and his "soul lost all heaviness." However, he did not agree with several religious principles promoted at the Startchetsvo and due to his pride, his conversations with Father Ambrose were often very tense and tiresome, despite the love that the latter surrounded him with.

All the meetings with people of different social classes and occupations accomplished day by day during almost thirty years regardless of the body weaknesses and suffering provided Starets Ambrose with true ascesis as though he were a recluse in the desert. He also managed to delegate skillful people and to guide them in charitable activities, especially for the sick, the orphans and the poor. Under his supervision a convent for nuns started to function in Shamordino, not far from Optina. Leo Tolstoy's sister, Maria, entered this convent in 1891. In his infinite love the Elder took also care of building an asylum, a school, a hospital and a hospice for unfortunate people. His devotion for the weak, the needy, and the suffering generated encouragement and peace. For them Optina became a "haven of hope and consolation."

Some people from those crowding the entrance at his cell had asked the Elder about the time of their death. Saint Ambrose said, "The Lord cuts short a man's life when He sees that either he is prepared to pass into eternity or that there is no hope left for him to change into a good person" (see Groza, 2016). At the age of 79, the Elder's body surrendered in its lengthy battle. Saint Ambrose reposed into the Lord on October 10, 1891, while he was still receiving people who came for advice and confession. He had predicted the day of his earthly death. A monk read the Canon of the Theotokos, next to Father Ambrose's bed, and then made a cross over the body of the ill Elder. The dying Father, with closed eyes, slowly raised his right arm to cross himself. He succeeded touching the forehead, the chest, and the right shoulder. He lost the last bit of energy, so his hand landed hard on his left shoulder as a result of his superhuman effort. Then he sighed three times and gave his soul to the Master of the universe. His face looked wonderful and bright, containing the expression of a warm, welcoming greeting.

A whole world wept at the news of his repose. Many people came to see him for the last time. It was very hot inside from all the burning candles. All of a sudden, droplets of sweat started to cover his forehead and a heavy stench spread in the whole chapel, quite repugnant to the visitors arrived for the farewell. The monks remembered that, when Father Ambrose was ill, he asked the others to read for him from the book of Job the details about how all the family ran away from Job's place due to the unbearable stink: "*I am repulsive to my wife, loathsome to the sons of my own mother…*" (*Job 19:17*). The Elder considered that he deserved a similar misery because during his life he had accepted many undeserved honors from others.

But before long, despite the fact that the air in the chapel became even hotter due to the crowds entering to see him, the body began to spread a sweet fragrance that remained all the rest of the days until after the funeral. Dostoyevsky described very accurately this "smell of corruption" in the above-mentioned novel, when he wrote about the death of his fictional character, Father Zosima. It is very astonishing for us to realize that this was Dostoyeky's premonition, because he finished his book ten years before the actual death of Father Ambrose.

Saint Ambrose was buried next to Elders Macarius and Leonid. At his grave the visitors could read Saint Apostle Paul's words: *"To the weak I became as weak, that I might win the weak. I have become all things to all men, that I might by all means save some"* (*1 Corinthians 9:22*).

Elder Anatole Zertsalov joined the Optina Startchestvo as a result of his prior miraculous healing from a devastating tuberculosis. Initially he labored spiritually under the guidance of Saint Macarius but later he became very close to Saint Ambrose. A fervent bearer of the Jesus Prayer, Father Anatole made such great spiritual progress that Saint Ignatius Brianchaninov at his visit at Saint John the Forerunner's Skete was deeply impressed and very happy for what he devotionally gained from the conversation with this Elder.

Starets Anatole was also a victim of the numerous attacks of the monks from the big Optina Monastery who disagreed with the hesychastic life of the Elders and their outstanding effect on the laypeople. However, he gladly received all these unfair adversities and used them for strengthening his spirit. This helped him because in the meantime he had joined the activities at the guesthouse. Being a great confessor, he was beloved by the pilgrims who always stopped first at his door before going to Father Ambrose.

Elder Anatole's deep humility and purity of soul was evident when he reacted with sincere suffering at the news that Saint John of Kronstadt saw him in a vision being surrounded by angels during the service of the Divine Liturgy. Although he became the Abbot of the Skete he continued to go for advice to Elder Ambrose, humbly kneeling at his bed, full of pious devotion. Gradually he achieved the same high level of spirituality as Saints Macarius and Ambrose. With his gift of clear discernment in assessing the thoughts and feelings of others, with his solid and subtle knowledge of the hidden aspects of the spirit, and even with an ease of foreseeing life events, Father Anatole was of a great help for his younger disciples and also for the lay people asking for counsel. Despite his weak health he went on pilgrimage to Kronstadt where he had the chance to serve the Divine Liturgy with the righteous Saint John of Kronstadt (1829-1909). Back at the Skete he received the Great Habit.

Elder Barsanuphius Plekhankov belonged to a rich family of Cossacks and had functioned as colonel in the military troops of Kazan before entering the small community of starets. As with many other Elders the decisive factor for changing his attitude from that of laity was also a miraculous healing from a fatal sickness from which he felt the fear of imminent death. He obeyed the vision ordering him to go to Optina. Arriving there he talked with Saint Ambrose who gave him some hints for preparation before joining the monastic community. He returned three months later but unfortunately it was the very day of Saint Ambrose's burial. Monk Barsanuphius made his apprenticeship under Elder Nectarius. As a Hieromonk he participated to the 1905-year war between Russia and Japan as a military chaplain. Back to Optina he found the Skete and its life very much deteriorated. He took over the position of Abbot and due to his energetic efforts the skete revived. Besides his administrative talents in relation to the others at the skete, Father Barsanuphius developed an intense spiritual labor as required by the hesychastic tradition of the place, and he eventually achieved great depth in ascesis and inner prayer. The activities at the Startchestvo again caused fierce opposition, and a strong group within the 300-brethren community of the big Optina Monastery battled to close the Saint John the Forerunner's Skete and to cast Abbot Barsanuphius away.

Starets Nectarius Tikhonov was one of the two last Elders of Optina and he had quite a peculiar personality. He grew within the great spiritual atmosphere of the Skete, under the careful guidance of Fathers Ambrose and Anatole. Cultivating a vivid talent for art, literature and science but remaining solidly anchored in the mystical background of the Starets, he thought for a while to go elsewhere as soon as he was ordained a Hieromonk. The Elders kept him at the Skete. Later he tried to live as a fool-for-Christ but the Elders stopped him from this new adventure. Eventually his temperament and aspirations found the best formula in a contemplative life in semi-reclusion where his soul achieved high spiritual levels. He restricted himself to his cell, firm in his decision to leave it only for the Church services and for his own funeral. He succeeded in controlling his thoughts, perfectly aware that they fly away and wander so easily and constantly in all kinds of worldy and spiritual thickets and traps. He recommended replacing free thinking with withdrawing into the inner universe of the soul for contemplation. Artists and writers are not real creators as they proudly claim because they are simply recombining in a different order images and words already created by the Lord, and they do so through the inspiration the Lord Himself put in them. The real art, Elder Nectarius said, is that of working on transforming oneself in the loving presence of God, through consistent labour in prayer, fasting and virtues.

On November 20, 1910, the Russian great writer Leo Tolstoy, a Christian anarchist excommunicated by the Church in 1901, died of pneumonia in the apartment of the chief of railroad station Astapovo. The Elders at Optina received the news of his last days with great dismay and Starets Varsonofy traveled in a hurry to Astapovo to talk with the dying man, who was being given injections of morphine. Unfortunately, the Tolstoyan associates surrounding the writer did not alow the Elder to take confession in order to prepare the suffering man's soul for its departure into eternity.

The other last Starets was Nikon Belyaev who worked under the guidance of Elder Barsanuphius and wrote down all the teachings of his master. The young Nicholas Belyaev was only nineteen when he came with his brother in 1907 to the Startchestvo. However, he already possessed an outstanding Christian background, received from his mother who was a spiritual daughter of the much-venerated Saint John of Kronstadt, and had been novice under the wise and loving care of the Metropolitan Tryphon Turkestanov from Moscow, good and closed spiritual friend with Father Barsanuphius. Metropolitan Trypfon was, on his turn, novice under Father Ambrose Grenkov of Oprina. Metropolitan Tryphon is the author of the beautiful Akathist of Thanksgiving ("Glory to God for All Things"). The Akathist was lost but found later in the cloths of the hieromartyr Grigori Petrov, deceased in a Siberian Gulag in 1940.

In 1909, after Elder Barsanuphius was exiled, monk Nikon had to leave the Skete and join the large community of the big monastery of Optina as a secretary. Elevated to the rank of Hieromonk in April 1917, only six months before the Socialist Revolution, Father Nikon succeeded in making the Monastery survive by reorganizing it into "an agricultural legion" after the Bolshevik authorities took away all its sources of income. The authorities abusively arrested Father Nikon in September 1917, threatened him and imprisoned him at Kozelsk, but after a time they let him go. Without giving up, Hieromonk Nikon returned to the Monastery to defend it, even with all the risk of exile or torture. He sheltered in Kozelsk the nuns chased away from Shamordino, the convent that was created and taken care of by the Staretchstvo. He also continued to receive, encourage and help the God-faithful refugees who were frightened, terrorized, and deprived by the new government.

The Monastery of Optina was closed in 1923 and vandalized in 1926. The authorities exiled Starets Nectarius to Kholminsk in Briansk District. He reposed there in holiness in 1928. At his reburial after seven years, his body was still intact and untouched by putrefaction. Father Nikon still strived to hold Divine Liturgy services at the deserted Optina Monastery and to host visitors until June 1924. He helped the needy and provided an oasis of hope, peace, and faith for all refugees - both exiled monks and laity. The unceasing practice of Jesus Prayer and the inner labour whose fire was never extinguished supported him in his devotional activities. The new atheist government arrested Father Nikon and other clergy members in June 1927. The following year he was exiled up north in the gulags of Solovki and Popov Islands in Karelia, then in camps near Archangelsk and Penega. He suffered with one leg that could barely move, and from tuberculosis. Eventually he exchanged his temporary life in this Valley of Tears for the eternal one in the Heavenly Kingdom on June 25, 1931 at the young age of forty-three. He departed from this world by making in the air the blessing sign of a big cross towards all his spiritual children far away.

In 1939 the buildings of Optina Monastery became a concentration camp for about eight thousand Polish officers captured during the Soviet Union's invasion of Poland. These men were part of the twenty-two thousand persons shot at the Katyn massacre in 1940. The Monastery served also as a military hospital and later, in 1944-1945, as a camp where the NKVD filtered Soviet prisoners liberated from the German camps. In 1987, in Gorbachev's Perestroika era, the Orthodox Church was allowed to reuse the Monastery's buildings which in the meantime functioned as an agricultural school. As a result, the

Monastery was restored in 1988 and Saint John's Hermitage was restored in 1990.

The long series of 14 Elders of Optina Skete looks like a divine constellation in the Russian Christian's sky. Its bright stars are the Starets Moses Putilof (1782-1862) and his brother, Anthony Putilof (1795-1865), Leonid Nagolkin (1768-1841), Macarius Ivanov (1788-1860), Ambrose Grenkov (1812-1891), Hilarion Ponamarov (1805-1873), Joseph Litovkin (1837-1911), Anatole Zertsalov (1824-1894), Isaac Antimonov (1810-1894), Barsanuphius Plekhanov (1845-1913), Nektarius Tikhonov (1853-1931), and Nikon Belaev (1888-1931). They were glorified by the Moscow Patriarchate in the year 2000. Their feast is the Synaxis of Optina Elders on October 11/24.

The majority of the information included in this chapter comes from the Synaxarion written by hieromonk Macarios of Simonos Petra Monastery at Mount Athos (see *The Venerable Fathers of Optina Hermitage...2018*) and from the article "Optina Pustyn: Spiritual Retreat of Tolstoy and Dostoyevsky" (Brumfield, 2014).

From the article "The Optina Elders and Their Sayings" (Rozhneva, 2014), it is good to learn some wise thoughts from the Elders: "If you somehow pardon someone sometime, for this you yourself will be pardoned" (Schema-Archimandrite Moses). "No one can offend us or irritate us if the Lord doesn't let this happen for our benefit, or as a punishment, or to try us and correct us" (Hieroschemamonk Macarius). "If you reconcile your heart to the one who is making you angry, then the Lord will tell his heart to be reconciled with you also...We must start everything that we do by calling on God's name" (Hieroschemamonk Hilarion). "If you notice a fault in a close one that you would like to correct, and this might destroy your peace of mind and annoy you, then you also are sinning and, consequently, you will not correct a fault by a fault—it is corrected by meekness... We ourselves aggravate our sorrows when we begin to complain" (Hieromonk Joseph). "

A sure sign of the deadening of the soul is evading church services. A person who has grown cold towards God first of all begins to avoid going to church—in the beginning he tries to arrive at the service a little late, and then he completely stops visiting God's church...Our whole life is a great mystery of God. All the circumstances of our life, however insignificant they may seem, have huge significance" (Hieroschemamonk Barsanuphius). "There is not, never was, and never will be a place on earth without sorrow. There can only be a place without sorrow in the heart, when the Lord is in it" (Hieroschemamonk Nikon).

The same author, Olga Rozhneva, mentioned the outstanding gifts of the Optina Elders achieved by the grace of the Lord: discernment, healing, foresight, powerful prayers. The elders knew the names of the persons they had not met, they read letters in sealed envelopes, and they named the sins forgotten by people during confession.

Starets Macarius' advices how to prepare for confession are a precious legacy and they are included in many Orthodox prayer books. Among other things Father Macarius teaches us that all the sins can be grouped in four categories: "we do not love God, we hate the neighbor, we do not trust the word and will of the Lord, we are full of pride and vain glory." If we would really have faith in God and we would sincerely listen to His teachings and commandments we would be aware of the eternal life and we would manage our life in a different way, far from the worldly matters which are shallow and perishable but enliven our heart and mind, fill us with ardent passion and hinder us from the vital work that our soul has to do during our short existence on earth.

Another thing that both Orthodox Christians from Russia and the whole world inherited from the Optina Elders is a beloved morning prayer that was said at Optina: "O Lord, grant that I may meet all that this coming day brings to me with spiritual tranquility. Grant that I may fully surrender myself to Your Holy Will. At every hour of this day, direct and support me in all things. Whatsoever news may reach me in the course of the day teach me to accept it with a calm soul and the firm conviction that all is subject to Your Holy Will. Direct my thoughts and feelings in all my words and actions. In all unexpected occurrences, do not let me forget that all is sent down from You. Grant that I may deal straightforwardly and wisely with every member of my family, neither embarrassing nor saddening anyone. O Lord, grant me the strength to endure the fatigue of the coming day and all the events that take place during it. Direct my will and teach me to pray, to believe, to hope, to be patient, to forgive, and to love. Amen."

In fact, this prayer was brought to Optina by Metropolitan Philaret of Moscow (1782-1867). It was probably written by Francois Fenelon, a French

Quietist author. Timothy Ware quotes another version in his book about the Orthodox Church (Ware, 1987).

Holy Elders of Optina, pray for us.

2.2. Paisianism in America.

2.2.1. Saint Herman of Alaska

According to Metropolitan Laurus (Laurus, 2004), the Paisian influence spread in three main directions in Russia: to the Northern (Valaam, St. Alexander Nevsky Lavra, and Solovetsky Monasteries), Central (Optina Hermitage, and monasteries in Moscow and Vladimir gubernyas), and Southern regions (Glinsky Hermitage). Saint Herman of Alaska, the Enlightener and Patron Saint of Orthodox America, learned about Saint Paisius' work on the Philokalia when he was a young monk at Valaam. As Schema-monk Metrophanes from Platina wrote, Saint Herman's "missionary zeal, love for the desert, practical application of patristic teachings, and his preoccupation with the Philokalia and the Jesus Prayer are all strikingly Paisian" (see *Little Russian Philokalia, vol. III*, 1989).

Saint Herman was born in Serpukhov, a region of Voronezh, probably in 1757. Raised in a pious merchant family, he bore the name Gerasimus. In their house there were books like the Holy Scripture, books about Lives of the Saints and those concerning Holy Fathers' teachings. Returning home from attending the Divine Liturgy, the large family used to sit together around the table for eating and always finished their meal by singing Psalms. Pilgrims on their way to the churches in Moscow or to Saint Sergius Lavra stopped sometimes by their house bringing with them pious words and songs that the children hidden in the corners of the room loved very much to hear. Saint Herman started his monastic life at twelve years of age when he entered the Sarov Monastery. His teachers were great Elders. Hieromonk Theodore Ushakov, who knew well Saint Tikhon and Saint Paisius of Neamts, was among them. Later, in 1778, the young monk Herman met the elder Cleopas, a former member of the Paisian community at Dragomirna Monastery in Moldavia. Father Gerasim Schmaltz who was the successor of Saint Herman in Spruce Island in Alaska, said that Saint Herman met personally Saint Seraphim of Sarov (see *Little Russian Philokalia, vol. III,* 1989).

Wishing to live a recluse life up north in the Roslav forest, Saint Herman entered the Valaam Monastery on Ladoga Lake under the spiritual care of Abbot Nazarius, in order to obtain his blessing to live as a hermit in the woods. The Abbot became his guide and Father, and after subjecting him to different obediences, he allowed him to start a hermit's life. Probably the Abbot knew that, because of his desire to retreat in solitude for being alone with God far from any distraction, Saint Herman had tried to flee twice at a younger age; one of his attempts was running to a very far Astrakhan region in order to cross the border into Persia. The hermitage where Saint Herman went after his noviciate under Father Nazarius was 1.5 miles far from the Valaam Monastery. Later this place became known as "Herman's field" (Germanovo, in Russian). The brethren of the monastery loved him for his humility and heart benignity, for his spiritual zeal and ardor. Metropolitan Gabriel of St. Petersburg tried twice to ordain him priest but he declined the offer due to his ardent desire of a simple monk's life in solitude.

While Saint Herman was still a teenager brother within the community of Valaam Monastery, an abscess grew on his throat and disfigured his face. It caused extreme pain, it gave off an unbearably bad odor and it barely allowed him to swallow when eating. He thought he would die. He locked the door of his cell and prayed with tears to the icon of Theotokos all the night. Eventually he used a wet towel to wipe the beautiful face of the Mother of God and he tied the towel around the abominable swelling. Deepened in his tearful, ardent prayer, he remained kneeling at the icon long hours until he felt down exhausted and entered a heavy sleep. He dreamed that Theotokos healed him with a loving touch. And it really was so because when he awoke the horrifying abscess disappeared, leaving only a small mark on his skin.

When he told the doctors about this healing, they did not believe it, "but the words of the physicians were the words of the weakness and inexperience of man in the face of the grace of God acting, and the order of nature being overcome" (see *Little Russian Philokalia, vol. III*, 1989). Metropolitan Gabriel asked Abbot Nazarius and Father Teophanes, the latter being an older companion of Saint Herman and under Saint Paisius's guidance for a period, to review and edit in Russian the "Dobrotoliubye" (Philokalia) published in Slavonic by Saint Paisius at Neamts Monastery. Philokalia became soon a very important book for the brethren of the monastery and encouraged them into a hesychastic life.

Metropolitan Gabriel of St. Petersburg led an intense overseas missionary activity. He intended to send the young monk Herman as a priest to the Russian Orthodox Mission in China. In the meantime, the Shelikhov-Golikov Company, active in Alaska, asked the Holy Synod of the Russian Orthodox Church to provide a priest for the native population. Tsarina Catherine the Great decided to send an entire mission to that region, entrusting the responsibility to Metropolitan Gabriel. Consequently, in 1793, ten monks from Valaam including Saint Herman were chosen, with the blessing of the Abbot Nectarius, for missionary work in Alaska. The whole group left Russia in 1794 and arrived on September 24, 1794, on Kodiak Island. Despite all difficulties they faced here, they succeeded to build a church and to baptize more than seven thousand Aleuts. Unfortunately, nine of the mission members died due to storms at sea, to martyrdom (Saint Juvenal) or to other causes. Only Saint Herman survived. After a period of time spent in the big island of Kodiak, where among other activities Saint Herman ran a mission school and taught agriculture, he decided to settle on Spruce Island, two miles far from Kodiak.

He lived first in an earthly cave and later during the winter in a small wooden cell built by the Russian American company. He planted a modest garden of potatoes, turnips, carrots and cabbage, fertilizing the crop with seaweed that he carried in buckets from the ocean. Later, when five poor families moved closer to his settlement, he enlarged the garden in order to feed all the hungry mouths. Life was harsh. His disciple saw him in a winter night carrying barefoot in the snow a log as big as only four strong people could carry. He bore a severe ascesis with much peace and serenity. The same soiled deer skin clothes winters and summers covered his body for more than eight years. He slept on a bench with two bricks for pillow and a wooden board for blanket. He was a relatively small man, ate very little, and because of all fasting and labor his body seemed very worn out and weak. However, God gave him strength to carry huge logs, besides the fifteen-pound chains with a cross he permanently had on him for increasing his striving of controlling the perishable flesh and liberating the spirit for adoration of the Lord. A recluse in his cell, with a very ascetic discipline of life and continuous prayer, Saint Herman suffered persecution for his faith with much stoicism.

Saint Herman of Alaska was a marvelous person. A warm smile illuminated his face which was surrounded by a very white beard and hair. He had bright lively blue-gray eyes but gradually lost sight as he grew older. Of a gentle and joyful nature, Saint Herman was gifted with a firm memory, quick mind, and good humor, and stood always open to talk and teach about faith in the Lord. Conversing with a soft, pleasant voice, he always went directly to the point, "in a business-like manner," making highly profitable every minute of discussion, as Schema-monk Sergius Yanovsky remembered.

Asked how he could stand such a life in loneliness under such harsh conditions, if not for its difficulty at least for its tedium, he replied, "I'm not alone there! There is God and God is everywhere! There are holy angels! With whom is it more pleasant and better to converse, angels or people? Angels, of course!" (see

Little Russian Philokalia, vol. III, 1989). Despite these words Saint Herman's love for people was immense, because as he said in his prayers, he considered himself "the humblest servant of the local peoples and their nurse." He visited the sick, brought peace and reconciliation to people arguing or fighting with each other, exhorted them for love, patience and repentance, and prepared dying people for their departure into eternity. He visited needy people and his spiritual son Yanovsky with much zeal and devotion; no rain, no storm, no snow, no completely dark nights could stop him from walking through the woods, meadows and rocky places to his destination. He welcomed everyone who knocked at his door but he did not let any person enter without a prayer. He built a small school for the children where he taught about God; he took care of the orphaned Aleut children.

He also loved the wild animals of the forest and lived with all of them in peace and mutual help. He talked to the bears and had a great friend in a bull that grazed in the meadow. Even the unfriendly ermines used to nest under his cabin looking for food from him. When his visitors or neighbors were hungry, he caught fish with bare hands and cooked it for them.

The Archpriest Prokopy Povarnitsyn said that one day Saint Herman fed his native guests with a little fish caught in the ocean; they ate until they were full, without taking into account the left-overs like those on the miraculous day recorded by Saint Evangelist Matthew (*14:17-21*) when our Lord Jesus fed the multitudes (see *Little Russian Philokalia, vol. III,* 1989). Saint Herman built also a little church dedicated to the Resurrection of Our Lord Jesus and, in remembrance of the monastery he came from, gave the name "New Valaam" to the whole eastern part of Spruce Island. As Archpriest Prokopy Povarnitsyn mentioned, Saint Herman served the Divine Liturgy inside that little wood building and sometimes the passers by or visitors could hear a choir singing during the service. If they wondered seeing him alone in the church, he gave them a logical and simple explanation – there were the angels who were singing with him!

When a big flood threatened the island, and the inhabitants were extremely frightened, the Elder encouraged them to trust the Theotokos as always in case of trouble and danger. He placed an icon of the Mother of God on a shallow ground and prayed for a long while. Then he said that the Holy Virgin would protect them all and the water would not exceed the very place where he put the blessed and powerful icon. Not much later, reality proved that he was totally right. Another time a huge fire started to spread in the woods of the island and again the Aleuts were frightened and ran to him asking for help. Saint Herman and his Aleut disciple Ignatius cleared a yard-wide strip at the foot of the hill, and prayed. The wild fire destroyed the woods up to that strip of upturned moss but, despite the wind and the power of the flames, it stopped there, without any damage beyond the clearing (see *Little Russian Philokalia, vol. III,* 1989).

Schema-monk Sergius (Simeon Yanovsky), who at thirty years of age was converted by Saint Herman from a free thinker to a true Christian, spent several years under his guidance. Eventually he left Spruce Island and returned to Russia. There he settled down at Optina Monastery, the other important hesychastic

Russian center besides Valaam, where a philokalic spirit and a Paisian approach of praying was predominant.

By an astonishing coincidence, Saint Herman left Russia in 1794, the year of the repose of Saint Paisius. He "arrived in America with a copy of the Paisian Philokalia" (see Metrophanes, 1994). The book became the favorite spiritual companion of Saint Herman. He kept it with him the rest of his life together with the book of Saint John Climacus. These things might be regarded as a beautiful continuity in the time and space of the spiritual toil and labor of the Holy Fathers: the hesychastic places in Moldavia and Russia, the work of Saint Paisius, the work of Saint Seraphim of Sarov and Saint Elders of Optina, the work of Saint Herman, and the spread of Orthodoxy in the New World. After WWII, elders from the Valaam and Optina Monasteries' spiritual line brought Saint Paisius' teachings to Jordanville and New-Diveyevo Convent. One can consider that Archbishop Averky, Archbishop Andrew (Father Adrian), and the Hierarchs Tikhon of California and Nektary of Seattle were also great Paisian personalities (see *Little Russian Philokalia, vol. III,* 1989).

Having the Slavonic Philokalia with him everywhere, Saint Herman was truly an "instructor of monks and converser with angels," as the Megalynarion says. He was especially fond of the Ladder of Teophanes that was included in the Philokalia and whose importance was often emphasized by Saint Paisius Velichkovsky. The ten steps of Theophanes' ladder are pure prayer, warmth of heart, holy energy, tears of the soul, peaceful thoughts, cleansing of the mind, mystical vision, mysterious illumination, penetration of light into the heart, and the imperfect perfection (see *Little Russian Philokalia* vol. III, 1989). He wrote in a letter dated June 20, 1820, "We, traveling on the journey of this life and calling on God to help us, ought to be divesting ourselves of this hideous garment and clothing ourselves in new desires... to receive knowledge of how near or how far we are from our heavenly homeland... One must follow the example of sick people, who, wishing the desired [health] do not leave off seeking means to cure themselves" (see *Little Russian Philokalia* vol. III, 1989).

A recluse in his cell, with a very ascetic discipline of life and in continuous prayer for himself and for the world, Saint Herman stoically suffered persecution for his faith from a few native pagan aggressors. A lover of justice, he did not hesitate to rebuke gently but firmly the authorities who oppressed the Aleuts and the disrespectful people who treated them with brutality. Sometimes, this caused anger, led to slander and made enemies for him. Based on false reports and complaints, the governor wanted to expel him from the island. Hearing the imaginary accusations, a priest, sent from Irkutsk (Russia), came with the governor of colonies and with local company workers to investigate Saint Herman.

They searched his cell and the surroundings for hidden currency and expensive goods. A zealous, hateful man, Ponomarkov, went further in his search. He took an axe and pulled out the boards of the floor. Saint Herman told him, "My friend, in vain have you taken this axe: this very tool will deprive you of your life!" And indeed, after a short while, when he and other workers were sleeping on a construction site, the Kenai natives beheaded him with his axe. Demons also bothered Father Herman as it happens with many holy men. Therefore, he said always preventively a prayer when saw somebody entering his cell.

Saint Herman reposed in 1837, on November 15 according to some historians (which coincides with the day of Saint Paisius' repose) or on December 13 or 25 according to other historians. He had instructed his spiritual son Gerasim, an Aleutian youth, what to do after the day of his death. He asked Gerasim to kill the bullock at once in order to avoid any suffering of his faithful animal friend. He desired to be buried next to his Aleut disciple Ignatius Aliaga, without waiting for the people from the Kodiak harbor who would not have been able to come anyway. He also wanted to have his head and face covered with the klobuk, and a cross set in his hands lying on his chest.

Surrounded by his orphans at the time of his repose, Saint Herman asked Gerasim to light candles at the icons and to read from the Acts of the Apostles. Then he gently leaned his head on Gerasim's chest and passed away. Immediately a sweet, heavenly fragrance filled the room. His face radiated a soft, transfiguring light – the light of Mount Tabor. When people from the Katari village in Afognak Island, a big island north of Kodiak and Spruce, saw, in the very evening of the repose, a column of bright light raising up to heaven from Spruce Island, they intuited at once that Father Herman had died and they started to pray for his soul.

The governor in Kodiak harbor heard the news of the saint's decease and ordered a fine coffin, planning to go right away to Saint Herman's place. However, as the holy man had said, a powerful storm started to stir the ocean, making impossible to cross the two-hour distance by boat for a month. Watched by the children, the dead body of Saint Herman rested in the cell until a local man finished making a simple coffin. The continuous heat inside the cabin did not alter the corpse at all. They buried the body as Father Herman wanted. The next day of his repose, the beloved bullock, full of sorrow and missing his master and friend, knocked a tree with his head and died (see *Little Russian Philokalia, vol. III,* 1989).

Five years later, Saint Innocent of Alaska (1797-1879), Archbishop of Kamchatka and the Aleutian Islands, future Metropolitan of Moscow, confronted in a boat a big, ferocious storm, not far from Spruce Island. Looking towards Saint Herman's place he prayed for help. The intercessory prayer was answered by God and the ocean quieted down. The great Saint Innocent, brilliant scholar and brave missionary, creator of the Aleutian alphabet and writing, descended on the land and served gratefully a panikhida (parastasos, memorial service) at Saint Herman's grave.

Ninety years after Saint Herman's repose, a monk came to the island exactly as the holy man predicted: Father Archimandrite Gerasim Schmaltz from Saint Tikhon of Kaluga's Monastery, near Moscow. Established in Afognak, Father Gerasim visited Saint Herman's desert place in 1927 immediately after Easter and served there a panikhida. Later that day, he left his companion and in his short, quiet, lonely break, he knelt next to Saint Herman's cabin. Full of joy, on such a sunny, festive day, he said, "Christ is risen,

Father Herman!" That very moment, the place was filled by a strong, sweet fragrance.

Five years later, Father Gerasim decided to settle in Spruce Island for good. Unfortunately, the local authorities and priest did not like this idea and threatened that if he was not going to leave the island on his own, they would force him out forced by the police. The night after receiving this sad news, Father Gerasim had a mysterious dream: while he was in a beautiful spruce forest a harmonious sound of bells like a song came from the direction of a clearing with lightly waving, velvety, tall grass. He saw a short monk, with a kind, smiling face, between two small trees. The monk told Father Gerasim that it was he, Saint Herman, who rang the Easter bells. He also encouraged Father Gerasim to have patience because all the threats would dissipate as though they never existed. This vision was depicted later in a beautiful icon of Saint Herman.

Father Gerasim moved in on September 8, 1935. Since Saint Herman's repose the place had remained unhabited for ninety years with a small exception – two families who made beer and caroused, but Saint Herman "drove them away." Father Gerasim erected a chapel on Saint Herman's site and lived there, alone, as a hermit. In his memories about the solitude of that meditative and prayerful place, Father Gerasim quoted a beautiful stanza: "The woods are silent, as in death;/ No sound the ear can capture/ Not even in the fleeting breath/ Of wind's consoling rapture." Father Gerasim had to leave the island in September 1965 after he became very sick due to a big tsunami caused by a powerful earthquake in March 1964 that covered his body with its freezing flood waters up to his neck. He reposed in Kodiak in 1969 (see Gerasim, 1989).

In conclusion, Saint Herman was Paisian by his missionary work, ascetic life, practical living of the patristic teachings, and his bearing of the mental prayer, the Jesus Prayer. God enriched him with the gifts of clairvoyance, healing, and discernment. The Troparion of Saint Herman goes as follows: "O blessed Father Herman of Alaska, North Star of Christ's holy Church, the light of your holy life and great deeds guides those who follow the Orthodox way. Together we lift high the Holy Cross you planted firmly in America" (See *Saint Herman of Alaska*, 1970).

2.2.2. Paisianism in Monastic Life.

The Holy Monastery of Saint Herman of Alaska was founded in 1970 by the monks Seraphim Rose and Herman Podmoshenski with the blessing of Saint Hierarch John Maximovitch, Archbishop of San Francisco, who belonged to the Russian Orthodox Church Outside of Russia. It is located in the Noble Ridge Mountain, at 3271 feet (997 m) elevation, above the unincorporated little village of Platina, in Shasta County, in northern California.

They continued the Paisian lineage brought from Russia on one side by Saint Herman of Alaska and on another side by their direct spiritual fathers Protopresbyter Adrian Rymarenko of New Diveyevo in New York State (Archbishop Andrew), Archimandrite Gerasim Schmaltz in Spruce Island (the follower of Saint Herman), Archimandrite Mitrophan in San Francisco (Saint John Maximovitch's friend),

Bishop Nektary Kontzevitch of Seattle (descendent of the Elders of Optina and temporary successor of Archbishop John Maximovitch) and his brother Professor Ivan Kontzevitch, a layman (see Christensen, 2003). The two young monks walked "in the steps of Blessed Paisius." They read his life and teachings with thirst for knowledge and with eagerness for a spiritual model. A Polish historian accurately noticed that Saint Paisius "referred approvingly to John Climacus" that "twosome or threesome monasticism, to be the best for novices" (Drozdek, 2014). "As Paisius and Bessarion, in the absence of a spiritual father" during their hermit period at Mount Athos, "had confessed their troubling thoughts to each other, so also did" the two monks, applying a "mutual obedience" in the first years when there were only the two of them in that remote place at Platina (Christensen, 2003).

Under the Abbots Herman Podmoshensky (1969-2000), Gerasim Eliel (2000-2009), Hilarion Waas (2009-2013), and Damascene Christensen (2013-present), the monastic community prospered and attracted many pilgrims. Since the year 2000 the St. Herman Monastery has been under the jurisdiction of the Western American Diocese of the Serbian Orthodox Church, protected with enthusiastic love by the young Bishop Maxim Vasiljevic. The Monastery pursues the founders' missionary activities in a Paisian spirit, by combining living in prayer and ascesis with publishing books and a well-received periodical journal entitled *The Orthodox Word*. The numerous writings of Father Seraphim Rose, a fervent defendant of the Holy Fathers' tradition, have been spread into the whole Orthodox Christian world and they have been very much welcomed even in the Eastern European countries with a long history of Orthodoxy, which liked his wisdom so much that they depicted him in icons. As Father Damascene Christensen (the author of a beautiful, massive, well-documented, popular biography of Hieromonk Seraphim Rose) mentioned, the books of the latter have been translated into Greek, Serbian, Romanian, Bulgarian, Georgian, Latvian, Polish, Italian, French, and Malayalam (a language in South India). Visiting Russia in 1998, Hieromonk Ambrose (formerly Father Alexey Young) found out that young people developed a great enthusiasm for these writings. They told him, "You know, Father Seraphim is really for us young *Russians*." Father Ambrose could not resist to reply, "That's funny; I always thought he was for us *Americans*" (see Christensen, 2003).

For many hermits, monks, and lay people living a righteous life, living intimately with the Lord in mind, heart and spirit is the fruit of being lovingly raised in a devoted Christian family. Sometimes God reveals His choice of messengers ahead of time even in the wombs of their mothers or in their first months of life. The holiness usually starts with a great suffering for the parents if the revelation occurs early (let us think of the beautiful example of Samuel narrated in 1 Kingdoms 1:11-18), or for the child (as in case of Saint Matrona of Moscow) or for the adult (as in case of Saint Mary of Egypt) if the revelation occurs later. The suffering might be the result of the painful detachment, like a tearing away from the preexistent sinful human structure, for entering a life of striving for purity, light, and blessing. Sometimes people decide to turn to God after a miraculous healing from a long, heavy illness or after rescue from a close encounter with death; in these cases, if a person had made a devotional promise in a prayer and God answered favorably, the promise would be repeatedly reminded to that person. Many great Optina Elders came to serve the Lord at the hermitage after a healing and a promise. In contrast with them, Father Seraphim Rose's road to God required a long, very dramatic, intellectual journey from the dark atheist pit of a Nietzschean unbeliever to the heights of light and faith. Eugene Rose wrote, "I was in hell, I know what hell is." Maybe, in a way, the Russsian martyr, theologian, philosopher, mathematician and scientist Father Paul Florensky went through a similar dramatic intellectual process.

Born in 1934 in a Protestant middle-class family in San Diego, Eugene Rose remained a Californian his whole life. Second-generation immigrants, his parents worked hard to make ends meet especially during the Depression era. A WWI veteran, of French and Dutch stock, his father, Frank Rose, was an unsophisticated "agreeable sort of fellow," ready "to take what comes in life" (Christensen, 2003).

His mother, of Norwegian origin, Esther Rose, born Holbeck, was a strong-willed wife, a Lutheran churchgoer, a businesswoman and an artist. His older sister, Eileen Rose, (who married a man with the last name of Busby), taught herself reading at three years of age and therefore she graduated the San Diego High School two years earlier, at age 16. Eugene was also very intelligent and studious. Gifted with an inclination for religion, he loved books and nature. In the Bible class at a Presbyterian church he easily memorized numerous scriptural quotes for his own delight. On his own initiative he was baptized and confirmed in a Methodist church at the age of 14. Of a fervent love for books and classic music Eugene found it easy to learn foreign languages; a teenager who was a possessor of "deep eyes" Eugene became a "lover of wisdom," as his High School colleague Walter remembered (Christensen, 2003).

The typical teenage striving to define himself marked Eugene deeply. He started as an enthusiastic non-conformist. Entering the philosophy department of the elite, private, liberal-arts Pomona College, he opened his eyes first on the West-European philosophers Spinoza and Nietzsche. The book *Thus Spake Zarathustra* that he read in the original German made a great impact on him.

Everything that was Christian in him was apparently erased and he became a fierce atheist. "But when Zarathustra was alone, he spoke thus to his heart: 'Could it be possible! This old saint has not heard in his forest that *God is dead*!'" (translation by R.J. Hollingdale). However, the passionate youth absorbed the "God is dead" saying without the wise discernment of Heidegger and others. He became adept at the nihilism that Nietzsche was afraid of, and deepened into great suffering and pessimism.

As his girlfriend Alison, an Anglican churchgoer, noticed, "Eugene recognized the existence of evil and error before he recognized the existence of good and truth" (see Christensen, 2003). She likened him with Ivan Karamazov, the turbulent and tragic character of Dostoyevsky's novel "Brothers Karamazov." For

Eugene, Ivan personified the Western intellectual who tries to explain and comprehend the essence of the material and spiritual world exclusively by his own mind and by his own logic; surely such an approach leads always to a status of doubting everything, which burdens the heart with heavy bitterness. Looking back to that time Eugene said, "to be a philosopher, not a professional or academic philosopher but a man for who to live is to think, means to suffer greatly" (see Christensen, 2003). An avid Nietzschean reader, Eugene Rose started to deal with the Antichrist, to feel his malicious, harmful presence and power. He forgot Nietzsche's words following his terrible affirmation, "God is dead; but given the way of men, there may still be caves for thousands of years in which His shadow will be shown."

However, Alison remembered how her friend cried, deeply shocked, everytime he was listening to Bach's Cantata "Ich habe genug" (I have enough). He felt in it the frightening thrill of death and, somewhere, the unseen, powerful presence of God. Eugene Rose heard a conference of the British philosopher Allan Wilson Watts, a promoter of Eastern thinking to Western media, who called the receptive youth to "The Way of Zen." Eugene decided to study the Chinese language, history and philosophy and he graduated in 1956, distinguished as magna *cum laude* student. He wrote, "Why does a person study religion? ... To find a reality deeper than the everyday reality that so quickly changes, rots away, leaves nothing behind and offers no lasting happiness to the human soul" (see Christensen, 2003). This thought sounds somehow like Mircea Eliade's idea of sacred and profane time, of the eternal time and perishable one (see Groza, 2016). In 1957 Eugene Rose attended the courses of Alan Watts at the American Academy of Asian Studies (today California Institute of Integral Studies) in San Francisco, on Zen Buddhism for realizing the man's true "self," but he was disappointed to find out that his professor used Zen for building a personal, comfortable and malleable religion. Continuing his Oriental philosophy studies, Eugene joined a master's degree program at the University of California at Berkeley. He learned the Mandarin language in order to read Chinese texts and graduated in 1961 with a thesis on the classical Chinese philosopher Lao Tzu, the author of the *Tao Te Ching*, a keystone writing for Taoism.

However, revelation came to Eugene Rose from another source. He declared, "It was René Guénon who taught me to seek and love the truth above all else." The French metaphysician René Guénon, undoubtedly the main promoter of the Traditional School (seconded by Ceylonese Ananda Coomaraswamy and French-Swiss Frithjof Schuon) was a scholar of large horizon. Developing the idea of Tradition, he searched for the Absolute Truth and the infinite Divine Presence that constitute the hidden (esoteric) and primordial core of all major religions of humankind. As Robin Waterfield in his book about Guénon wrote, "Tradition was essentially that body of knowledge and self-understanding which is common to all men of all ages and nationalities... It is supra-temporal in origin, the link which unites man as manifestation to its unmanifest origin" (Waterfield, 1987). At the same time "Tradition is analogous to the Logos or uncreated word emanating from the Gottheit [(the Godhead, the state of being God, the very substance of God, the Divinity)] of Eckhardt" and it refers to what "is the invisible link between manifest universe, including man, and the Ultimate Reality, the Principial Truth which sustains it and from which the world derives" (Waterfield, 1987). René Guénon had his limits. He "could not bring himself to accept that the highest form of knowledge was to be obtained by the union of the mind and the feelings, the union of the intellect with love. This being so... he insisted on following his lonely path of pure intellectual intuition" (Waterfield, 1987). However, he could not remain in a metaphysical sphere above all beliefs and philosophies, he needed something more concrete and better defined in order to live in it and therefore he eventually adhered to Sufism, the esoteric, mystical dimension of Islam, for a more authentic contemplative life.

Eugene Rose also discovered the very important writing of the Sufi European leader Fritjof Schuon, *The Transcendent Unity of Religions*, published in 1953. According to this author it is possible to transcend all traditions into a unique universal esoteric interpretation (comprehension). The seventh chapter, *Christianity and Islam*, and especially the eighth, *Universality and Particular Nature of the Christian Religion*, made many people who were attracted by Sufism at that time to turn to the Orthodox Christianity which Fritjof Schuon and René Guénon considered the most authentic, "the purest form of Christian Tradition."

As the French-Swiss thinker said in an interview in 1995, "all [authentic religions] are right, not in their dogmatic [exoteric] exclusivism, but in their unanimous [interrelated] inner signification, which coincides with pure metaphysics [(or accedes to)], or in other terms, with the *philosophia perennis*." Schuon affirmed that every religion is characterized by a related esoteric dimension, "which is essential, primordial and universal." Eugene Rose's interest in Orthodoxy increased after he read this book. He also noticed an "outward similarity between Jesus Prayer described in Philokalia and the Shinshu Buddhist prayer to the Amida Buddha called the 'recitation of the Divine Name'" (see Christensen, 2003).

Thinking of his previous nihilist, atheist conviction, Eugene Rose confessed, "When I knew the Antichrist must exist, I knew that He whom Antichrist opposes also must exist. I knew that Christ must exist." He also realized that "Truth was not just an abstract idea [like in atheism], sought and known by the mind, but was something personal – even a Person – sought and loved by the heart." He concluded: "that is how I met Christ" (see Christensen, 2003). Finally, Eugene Rose understood the Personal aspect of God and the fact that by prayer one can have and live an intimate dialogue person to person. Any exploration, avoiding the awareness of God's will that is manifested in the whole universe, leads to hell. In an imaginary *Answer to Ivan Karamazov* (see Christensen, 2003) Eugene Rose wrote, "We know existence is suffering and we know that our God loves us and for this love suffered even more intensely than the great Saints; we know this, and yet we presume to 'doubt', to offer our petty questioning of the 'meaning' of it all. O vile man! Accept it and suffer more, and pray to God – pray for no object, for no cause, merely give your heartfelt prayers and tears to Him. He knows the 'why' of it. He knows all." Eugene Rose decided to write down all the conclusions from his spiritual exploration in a massive book of "religious philosophy" entitled *The Kingdom of Man and The Kingdom of God*, with very well-structured contents; unfortunately (or fortunately?) he never finished it. Eugene's first direct contact with the Orthodox Church was at Vespers at the Russian Cathedral Joy of All Who Sorrow in San Francisco, when the crippled, bent-over Archbishop Tikhon Troitsky was serving. He attended later with much emotion the service of Good Friday and of the Great Feast of Holy Resurrection. When Bishop John Shahovskoy said in Russian the Paschal greeting, "Christos Voskrese" (Christ is risen), he answered joyfully together with all the others, "Vaistinu Voskrese" (Indeed He is risen).

This is how Eugene Rose came out of the dark, stumbling portion of his long spiritual journey for which he paid with much suffering. Now he was walking straight, in light, with a rejoicing heart and a deeper understanding of Lord's teachings. *"The law of the Lord is blameless, converting souls; the testimony of the Lord is trustworthy, making children wise; the ordinances of the Lord are right, rejoicing the heart; the commandment of the Lord is bright, enlightening the eyes"* (*Psalm 18/19: 8-9*).

Let us not praise the man; the confidence in him and the ignorance or denial of God lead to doubting and despair. *"Not to us, O Lord, not to us, but to Your name give glory, for Your mercy and Your truth; lest the nations say 'Where is their God?' Our God is in heaven above; and both in heaven and on earth, all things whatsoever He wills, He does."* (*Psalm

113/114,115:9-11). *"He who abides in Me, and I in him, bears much fruit,"* said Christ Our Lord to His disciples (*John 15:5*).

During the Christmas break of 1959, Eugene Rose visited his parents at their new home in Carmel and bade farewell to his girlfriend Alison. The decision was made: he would dedicate his life to the Lord in a monastic way. His loving biographer Father Damascene inserted a beautiful poem at the beginning of that chapter of his book: "I cannot raise my eyes to yours;/ I cannot lift my lowered head,/ Nor speak those words which might be said./ But when the wind of autumn stirs/ The dying leaves, and we must part,/ We'll hold some meaning in the heart:/ Unspoken, since we both believed/ In Him Who in His love has brought/ From out of silence, out of naught,/ The universe that He conceived" (Damascene Christensen: *Silence*; in Christensen, 2003).

In 1961 Eugene Rose met Gleb Podmoshensky in San Francisco. He was a recent graduate of the Orthodox Seminary at Holy Trinity Monastery in Jordanville, New York. Gleb's birthplace was the city Riga in Latvia. After his father died in the communist gulags, his mother defected with him and his sister from the Soviet Union during the German invasion in WWII. From West Europe Gleb immigrated into United States with his relatives in 1948. The friendship with Gleb was decisive for Eugene Rose.

In February 1962 Father Nicholas Dombrovsky at the Joy of All Who Sorrow Cathedral delivered the Chrismation Sacrament to Eugene who thus entered the Church as a true Orthodox believer. It was the day of his holy patron, Saint Eugene of Alexandria and, by a wonderful coincidence, the Sunday of the Prodigal Son. His godparents were Gleb's friend Dimitry Romanov and his wife, both of strong, deep faith lived in total simplicity and unaffectedness, despite their Russian/French blue blood (*"Blessed are the poor in spirit, for theirs is the kingdom of heaven"* - Matthew 5:3). Eugene already had meditated on the tradition of Church that he now fully accepted. He wrote that is is not for us to choose "what is important and what is dispensable… We as Orthodox Christians are not free to deny [the tradition of Church] or reinterpret it, but must believe as the Church hands it down to us, with simplicity of heart" (Christensen, 2003).

Saint John Maximovitch, the Archbishop of San Francisco, liked the new zealous convert and took Eugene under his holy and patient guidance. In 1963 the Archbishop John Maximovitch gave Eugene Rose and his friend Gleb Podmoshensky the task to work with their juvenile enthusiasm in spreading the Orthodox Faith through books and publications. With his blessing they formed a missionary brotherhood, choosing Saint Herman of Alaska as its patron Saint, because they saw in the latter the first missionary who brought the Orthodox Faith to the American land. The St. Herman of Alaska Brotherhood opened a bookstore next to the new Cathedral in 1964 and created the St. Herman Press publishing house in 1965 which issued a journal, "The Orthodox Word."

Archimandrite Gerasim Schmaltz who followed Saint Herman's steps in Spruce Island found a brass icon of the Mother of God "Joy of All Who Sorrow" on the beach. The icon belonged to Saint Herman. Father Gerasim sent it to the young founders of the

Brotherhood. Gleb Podmeshensky went in 1961 to Spruce Island where he stayed for a long while with Father Archimandrite Gerasim, collecting all the stories about the miraculous healings made by Saint Herman's intercessory prayers; later he even visited some of those persons for more revelatory details.

The veneration of Saint Herman has been always very intense and thousands of pilgrims have visited his chapel in Spruce Island every year. I cannot resist repeating one story already mentioned in a previous book (Groza, 2016). A faithful woman asked her husband to bring a little water from Saint Herman's spring. The man believed in God, belonged to a Protestant church, and was a nice person.

He traveled to the island where the Saint had lived. When he arrived at the spring that had a miraculous power of healing, he realized that he forgot to take a clean bottle for the water. So, he drank all the wine from the bottle he carried in his backpack and tried to fill it with the blessed water of the spring. To his and all the others' great surprise, when he dipped the bottle in the spring, the water became dirty, strangely colored and totally undrinkable. This thing frightened all the people present and since then everyone has approached the spring with great respect. This is quite a clear warning about the danger of the liberties that we are sometimes tempted to take while handling sacred things. The Orthodox Church is kind and gentle with everyone's weaknesses, but we are not allowed to make our own rules, disregarding the Church's recommendations. The Church's Saints often attention us with delicate care on this aspect. At the advice of Saint John Maximovitch, the two young apprentices

Eugene and Gleb commited themselves to a monastic life and decided to transform the brotherhood into a real monastic community. Consequently, in 1967, with Eugene Rose's parents' help who covered the downpayment cost, the two young friends bought a place in the Northern California wilderness, in the Noble Ridge Mountain area, near Platina. Because both were psalmists at the San Francisco Cathedral and one at least had to be present, they could not go together to work at their projected monastic settlement in that remote area. They took turns. Podmoshenski was the first to spend a week alone in the woods. He fought with the roughness of the nature of month of May. He had moments of fear and loneliness and went alternatively through states of enthusiasm and deep discouragement.

However, he never stopped praying. Fixing their little shack, he realized all of a sudden that there was no cross on the place. He nailed one together but it came out bigger than he expected. He could barely carry and drag it to the chosen spot, stumbling often under its heavy weight. He soon became exhausted, suffering under the cold rain that was unceasingly pouring down in the deep silence of the mountain. He was carrying his cross! Because he did not have a shovel it was hard to dig in the compact, rocky soil. At the end of his endurance, he prayed and decided anyway to try to erect the cross in the tiny, 6-inch-deep hole he dug. He made a huge effort to lift the cross and, singing the Prayer of the Cross, he let it slide into the hole. A miracle happened. The cross did not fall! It stood there as "suspended in the air or held by invisible angels" (see Christensen, 2003). The rain intensified and continued the whole night "with winds howling and echoing all over the forest." That night the future monk Herman had a dream: a big crowd was marching and he was in it, side by side with the Archbishop John Maximovitch. He knelt and, kissing the holy man's hand, he humbly asked for his blessing. The Archbishop looked straight in the youth's eyes and silently thanked him for erecting a cross in the wilderness. Waking up, Gleb realized that it was the very day of May 7, when 1616 years ago, in 351 A.D., a brighter-than-the-sun image of a cross appeared in the morning in the sky of Jerusalem, stretching all the way from the Mount of Olives to Golgotha, a distance of about five and a half miles. It was, as Father Seraphim said later, like "bringing Orthodoxy to the land of cowboys" (Christensen, 2003).

Responding to the inner call of their great religious fervor, the two enthusiastic friends began in 1968 an ascetic life at Platina place. They were tonsured by Archbishop Artemon in the presence of Bishop Nektary, a spiritual son of St. Nectarius of the Optina Startchestvo, on a sunny, calm day in October 1970, after a string of ten penitence-like rainy, windy days. Eugene Rose received the monastic name of Seraphim after Saint Seraphim of Sarov and Gleb Podmoshensky received the name of Herman after the holy patron of their Brotherhood. They continued to consider themselves disciples of Saint John Maximovitch and firmly believed that his words about a "missionary monastery in California" like "a reflection of Valaam" and Valaam's Abbot, Father Nazarius, represented Saint John Maximovitch's testamentary will for St. Herman Monastery.

In 1975 the two monks Seraphim and Herman published the first book at the St. Herman of Alaska Monastery. The book considered the lives of "the desert-dwellers of the Russian forests," including the great Saint Sergius of Radonezh, and the "angel-like" holy men Saint Cyril of White Lake and Saint Nilus of Sora (Christensen, 2003). The title of the book, "The Northern Thebaid" was inspired by the existence of the ancient Thebaid of the Desert Fathers of Egypt. Compiling and editing it the brethren Seraphim and Herman put together something that became food for the soul and guide for their further monastic life in the desert of the Noble Ridge mountain.

After this first step was completed as a spiritual foundation, the two monks published the *Life of Saint Paisius Velichkovsky*, the creator of the modern line of monastic and desert-dwellers that comes up in time from the 18th to the 20th century. Because of Saint Paisius' work of copying, translating, editing and promoting the Philokalia, a collection of the Holy Fathers' teachings about the Jesus Prayer, they thought that publishing a book about the life and writings of this particular Saint could help them to find an easier, faster and more essential way to connect themselves to the spiritual masters from the 4th to 15th centuries. Father Seraphim emphasized the importance of such a book: "The life of Blessed Paisius is of special value to us because it is the Life of a Holy Father of modern times, one who lived like the ancients almost in our own day" (see Metrophanes, 1994).

Father Seraphim wrote the introduction to the book about Saint Paisius, thinking of a teenager named Gregory who scared his parents with his rebellious attitude and ran away from home in great anger. In his wide wandering he found love and warm understanding at Saint Herman Monastery. Enjoying his new shelter and grateful to his hosts, he paid them back by building a shack for storing what was printed in the monastery. They called it, with appreciation, the "Gregorian Hall." They also introduced Gregory to a more spiritual life, with trust and love for the Church, bringing to his attention the spiritual zeal Saint Paisius had at the age of 17—Gregory's age at the time. Today, Father noted, the "paganized modern life" negates the moral and spiritual upbringing of young people. It is necessary therefore to act immediately, without any procrastination, at this still early age, to correct the present deficiencies of upbringing and of social environment, before it's too late. Father Seraphim wrote in his introduction to the book of Saint Paisius' life, "Let us then struggle while it is still day, with the time and the weapons which All-merciful God has given us!" We find here the same awareness of the unforgiving time flow, the same imperious need to enter as soon as possible the right and straight way, Saint Herman of Alaska formulated to the sailors, "For our own good, for our own luck, let us at least promise that <u>from this very day, very hour, very minute</u>, we shall try to love God more than anything else and to obey to His Holy Will!"

The book published at Platina was well received by the Orthodox world. In Greece it was translated and published in 1990, as had happened with the previous book issued by St. Herman Brotherhood, *The Northern Thebaid*. Unfortunately, Fathers Seraphim and Herman did not succeed in accomplishing their whole project:

the first volume about Saint Paisius' life (see Metrophanes, 1976) was not followed by the second, about Saint Paisius' writings. It remained the task of their successors to publish the teachings about prayer and monastic life teachings. Consequently, the second volume was published later, in 1994, but under a different form (see *Little Russian Philokalia*, 1994a).

People wanted to read and learn more from the lives and wisdom of the Russian anchorites and hermits who shared the Paissian spirit, for example Elders Anthony of Optina and Zosima of Siberia living in the forest of Roslavl. Another 17-year-old teenager at this time, also named Gregory but a desert-lover with a strong faith in God, visited Platina Monastery and, because he was quite familiar with the Russian language, the Fathers asked him to work on converting the original texts into English. Another desert-lover, Barbara McCarthy, a previous opera singer, the future Mother Brigid at Saint Xenia Skete, offered her help to transcribe the translations. Thus, two more books were issued: one about the life of Elder Zosima of Siberia and the other about the life of his disciple, Peter Michurin. These triggered a whole series under the name of Little Russian Philokalia, in which the life and work of Saints Paisius Velichkovsky, Seraphim of Sarov, and Herman of Alaska were included.

In 1977 the two monks were ordained Hieromonks by Bishop Nektary of Seattle. Now they could celebrate the Divine Liturgy at the Monastery. As a result, the monastic community grew and so also did the multitude of pilgrims. *"If you keep My commandments, you will abide in My love, just as I have kept My Father's commandments and abide in*

His love... You are My friends if you do whatever I command you," Our Lord Jesus Christ said (*John 15:9 and 14*). The Fathers' fervor of living Christ's teachings, their intense life of prayer and their wisdom acquired from Holy Scripture and the Holy Fathers' writings made the Platina place a blessed one, attracting numerous people thirsty for God who came to attend the services and ask for Father's counsel.

The practice of Jesus Prayer became for the Paisian-in-spirit monastic community members the daily support of their minds and hearts, fed their souls with the awareness of God's presence and love, and helped them in their spiritual podvig. Father Seraphim and the other brethren said this prayer when they were not at the Church services: while working, while walking, while resting. They also respected the ancient monastic habit of saying it every time they entered a room. Fathers Seraphim and Herman followed the "Optina Five-hundred" rule of prayer: 300 Jesus Prayers, 100 prayers to Theotokos, 50 to the Guardian Angel and 50 to All Saints (Christensen, 2003).

However, they knew the risks of being shallow in this prayer. Father Seraphim warned the brethren that in the podvig (or "the unseen warefare" in Nicodemus of the Holy Mountain's terms), it is important to pursue "the emotional development of the soul." Striving for "an elevated state of prayer" is fruitless without building the ability "to respond to normal human love and friendship; for '*If a man say, I love God, and hateth his brother, he is a liar; for he that loves not his brother whom he hath seen, how can he love God Whom hath not seen?*'(*1 John 4:20*)" (see Christensen, 2003). In a sermon held in the refectory for the brothers and pilgrims, Father Seraphim told the story of a zealous person in San Francisco who imposed upon himself the rule of saying the Jesus Prayer five thousand times every morning before starting any activity. He said it on the balcony of his house in the middle of the city and every time after finishing the whole series "he felt wonderfully refreshed and inspired." It happened one day that somebody stopped under his balcony and began working there very noisily. The praying person became angry and, interrupting his last thousand Jesus Prayers, started throwing dishes at the man doing the work. Father Seraphim commented, "This means that inside of him the passions were free, because he had some kind of deceived idea or opinion that he knew what was right for himself spiritually... In this case it is more profitable not to say those 5,000 Jesus Prayers, but to do something else that is spiritual" (see Christensen, 2003).

Let us remember that Saint Paisius Velichkovsky indicated different stages of prayers for the different degrees of spiritual strength of the monastic brethren. In a similar way, Father Seraphim wrote to a young pilgrim, "If you still accept my authority as a spiritual father, I am giving you a different prayer rule: instead of the Jesus Prayer, say every night 100 prayers by the prayer rope, with words something like this (or the equivalent in your own words): 'Lord Jesus Christ, have mercy on my brother (name)'... going by name through all the people close to you, starting with your immediate family. With each petition make a bow (prostrations for members of your immediate family). Stop at 100 (repeating names if necessary) and let your last petition be for everyone. By this I want you to wake up and start loving your brothers and sisters, both of the household of faith and those without" (quoted by Christensen, 2003).

Fasting was an important part of their ascetic life. Its rule did not mark strictly the periods established by Church as fasting periods because it did not allow a return to a careless way of living in the nonfasting time. Each new fasting period added another gain in climbing the ladder to the spiritual heights. The vigilance learned and practiced in those periods also continues its effect after the fasting is over. "Don't waste what you have been given," Father Seraphim used to say, as a spiritual son of Bishop Nektary. "Don't spill the grace. Keep it there!" (see Christensen, 2003).

The fact that the day of Saint Herman's repose (November 15, 1836) coincided with Saint Paisius' day of repose (November 15, 1794) increased the affectionate attachment to the Ukrainian Saint. The monks of Saint Herman's Monastery called a hill in the area "The Paisian Hump." Archbishop John Maximovitch promised the monks of Saint Herman's Monastery a much-desired list of Romanian saints and disciples of Saint Paisius. Veneration for Saint Paisius affected many aspects of the monastic life as well. They welcomed every visitor and any person who wanted to join them, respecting the tradition established by Saint Paisius who always considered that the person who comes to him should never be cast out because "another brother is another prayer." A strong emphasis was put on frequent confession, which Saint Paisius recommended during his time: "Everyone, and above all beginners, was to confess his thoughts each evening to his spiritual father". The rule of "revelation of [hidden] thoughts" set the confession as a "foundation of true repentance and forgiveness of sins." This strengthened the control of the person confessing and the discipline of the spirit. Saint Paisius, while being Abbot at the Romanian Monastery of Dragomirna, instituted the habit of gathering the brethren every evening in the trapeza (refectory) for reading from Patristic writings. This habit became also a rule at Platina.

The Divine Liturgy on the Feast of the Transfiguration in August 1982 was the last liturgy Father Seraphim served. Immediately after that he fell sick with atrocious pain in his stomach. The Monastery brethren insisted on taking him to the hospital in Redding, against his will. Finding out the real cause of the illness, the doctors wondered how stoic Father Seraphim has been, taking all the excruciating pain without any complaining. Blood clots stopped the blood flow to the intestines and part of those started to become gangrenous. The surgeon removed the dead tissue. However, back in the ICU room, Father Seraphim could not resist the pain anymore. He became delirious and lost control of his body under the devastating torture of his condition. He steamed out floods of curses, threats, vindicative words, like in a dreadful battle with demons.

A second operation was necessary. Much weaker, Father Seraphim was now more serene, more at peace, as his disciples knew him. He could not speak but tried to make Father Herman understand that he saw in his agony Saint John Maximovitch, their beloved Archbishop and Teacher, who consoled and encouraged him, breathing peace into his body and spirit. Fearing that they would lose Father Seraphim soon and that the long dreamt-of project, as a solemn promise, to build a skete together on Spruce Island at Saint Herman's site would remain unfinished, Father Herman asked, "If you die, do you bless us to go there to continue St. Herman's New Valaam?" With a huge effort Father Seraphim raised his fingers in a sign of blessing.

Hundreds of lay people came to see him, to talk to him and to pray for his recovery. During his whole week of suffering, the Divine Liturgy was served every day at the hospital's chapel. Long and ardent prayers were said with tearful eyes at the St. Herman's Monastery before the wonder-working Icon of the Mother of God, "Quick-Hearer." The monks at the Docheiariou Monastery on Mount Athos were also praying to this Icon for Father Seraphim's healing. With the I.V. tubes and wires of monitoring devices all over his body, tied to the bed to prevent his movement in case of seizures, and with a respiration mask on face, Father Seraphim looked like a martyr, crucified by the world with its frightening technology.

Bishop Nektary, the Optina descendant who loved Father Seraphim very much, came to visit his spiritual son, made a continuous vigil and officiated in the chapel with long prayers of supplication. Eventually he told Father Herman, "Be prepared. Perhaps Father Seraphim is now ripe for the heavenly kingdom." Later Father Herman gave him Communion and read the Gospel over the Father's dying body. Unexpectedly, Father Seraphim raised himself with a huge effort, kissed the Bible and then fell down on bed, exhausted. His eyes and all the others' in the room were in tears.

On September 2, 1982, Father Seraphim reposed after a week of suffering. His mouth remained in perpetual gentle smile and one could read a perfect peace and a soft light emanating from his face, like a sign from the Heavenly Kingdom. He departed from this word under the aura of the Theotokos' Dormition Feast period (before the Leave-taking on September 5, according to the old Russian Church's calendar). He was still very young when he departed from this life: only 48 years old.

During the dramatic week of Father Seraphim's suffering in the hospital, two persons had in their dreams the premonition of his imminent departure from this world: Helen Kontzevitch, professor Ivan Kontzevitch's wife, who envisioned a far-away, enigmatic person singing the heavenly magnification hymn to the Theotokos with Father Seraphim's tenor voice; and Alison, his former girlfriend, who saw him ill, bedridden, in agony, wishing to talk to her but unable to articulate a word.

Father Seraphim's inert body was brought back to the monastery to be buried. Weeping and praying next to his coffin in the church, Ellie Anderson, a spiritual daughter, smelled a bad odor and had the impression that she heard Father Seraphim's anguished voice saying, "I'm rotting, I'm rotting." She looked at the coffin and to her relief saw Father's quiet face, reflecting infinite peace, while the odor became "sweet, like that of roses" (see Christensen, 2003). Is this not a reminder of a similar moment at Elder Ambrose's repose? The soul's journey in the life beyond this material world includes the undressing from the known and unknown sins. *"Who will understand his transgressions? Cleanse me from hidden sins*" (*Psalm 18/19:13*). Thinking of Elder Ambrose's words about the Lord's decision on the length of life of each of us, and mourning for Father Seraphim's presence of only 48 years among us, it is good to repeat the quote that the excellent, sensitive and loving biographer, Father Damascene, made from the Holy Scripture: "*He, being made perfect in a short time, fulfilled a long time: for his soul pleased the Lord; therefore hasted He to take him away from among the wicked*" (*Wisdom of Solomon 4:13-14*).

At the time the crowds were passing to say goodbye to the deceased while hymns were sung, the same spiritual daughter of Father Seraphim saw his image, dressed in bright and clean monk's clothes censing the altar. Bishop Nektary consoled a nun with the words: "Don't pray *for* Father Seraphim, pray *to* him" (see Christensen, 2003). His intercessory help became evident through the cases of miraculous healing and problem solving which were recorded by the faithful people after his repose.

Saint Paisius' Monastery. In April 1991, on Bright Friday (the first Friday after Pascha), the Feast Day of Theotokos' Life-Giving Spring, the Saint Paisius Abbey of nuns in Forestville, California, opened its gates to pilgrims. Under the spiritual guidance of Saint Herman Brotherhood from the monastery in Platina, the Saint Paisius Missionary School held periodic conferences, courses, and commemorations for the very much-needed education of the young Orthodox generation. A service of blessing the waters invested the grounds of the abbey with a special godly call, under the sign of the Icon of the Mother of God the "Quick Hearer," a blessed copy from the original existing at Mount Athos. The abbey, keeping the Paisian monastic rules with daily services, was dedicated to translating, editing, and publishing patristic literature, as Saint Paisius used to do at Neamts and Dragomirna. The second English edition of the biography of Saint Paisius, written by Father Metrophanes, was published at the abbey in 1994 (the first was at Platina in 1976), in addition to his writings "The Scroll" and "The Field Flowers" included in the *Little Russian Philokalia*, vol. IV.

This beginning marked a large window into Romanian monastic spirituality. A special issue of *The Orthodox Word* of 1992 talked about the tradition of Saint Paisius Velichkovsky in Romania and in contemporary America, and presented Forestville Abbey, that had a beautiful Moldavian wooden gate and was located "in a quiet mountain area like the Moldavian Mountains." This particular issue made the connection with the Paisian line and several great Romanian monastic personalities like Father Cleopa Ilie from Sihastria Monastery and Paisius Olaru from Sihla Skete (see *The Tradition of St. Paisius Velichkovsky...*, 1992). The Abbey translated into English and published in 1996 the first volume of the Romanian Patericon written by Father Ioanichie Balan, and in 1997 the book *Christ Is Calling You* by Father George Calciu-Dumitreasa.

The two-hundred-year commemoration of the repose of Saint Paisius was celebrated at the abbey in 1994. A special conference was dedicated to the golden chain of holiness in Romania – the predecessors and the successors of Saint Paisius Velichkovsky. *The Orthodox Word* (see *The Bicentennial of St. Paisius Velichkovsky*, 1994) published narratives from Saint Paisius' life as they were written in the *Chronology of Neamts Monastery* by Andronicus the Confessor and also an Akathist to Saint Paisius, written by two young monks from the Skete on Spruce Island where Saint Herman made his blessed podvig of deification. It is a wonderful thing to see how the patristic tradition is propagated over the centuries, and how it ties together important sites of deep spirituality and hesychastic labor. The present generations have the responsibility of maintaining this continuity.

Gradually the sisterhood increased as number of nuns. The official year of the monastery's foundation was 1993. Its home school bore the sign of the Protection of Theotokos. The nuns from Saint Paisius Abbey in Forestville moved in 2001 to Safford, Arizona, in the high desert, where a new Saint Paisius Monastery was established, under the ruling bishop Maxim of the Serbian Western American Diocese. Today the coenobitic community has twenty nuns. They continue to publish books and akathists, have a large bookstore, make prayer ropes, labor in the vegetable garden and the olive and fruit orchards, and grow a flock of milk goats for maintaining a self-sufficient status and for hosting thousands of visitors.

Conclusions

Yes, it is more attractive to eat, to drink, to dance, to be merry. To satisfy all our desires and needs in a decent and honorable way without harming others is not a sin. However, *"life is more than food, and the body is more than clothing"* (*Luke 12:23*). We leave our heart unanswered in her true desires - we forget the need and the joy of salvation. "The desires of the human heart cannot be satisfied with the goods of this world, because only the grace of God can quench the thirst of our desires," noticed Saint Innocent of Alaska (quoted by Belonick, 1989). Saint John of Kronstadt warned us: "Our heart dies spiritually every day; only ardent, tearful prayer can restore it [back] to breath and life" (quoted by Belonick, 1998). Therefore, "if we make every effort to avoid death of the body, still more should it be our endeavor to avoid death of the soul. There is no obstacle for a man who wants to be saved other than negligence and laziness of soul," as Saint Anthony the Great adviced (*The Philokalia*, 1982).

We have to seek God. He is the source of our true life, the life of our soul. Yes, *"no one has ever seen God"* the Father (*John 1:18*). Nevertheless, we have to find Him. *"Moses drew near the thick darkness where God is"* (*Exodus 20:21*). "This is called darkness by the Scripture, which signifies, as I said, the unknown and unseen," wrote Saint Gregory of Nyssa (quoted by Staniloae, 1998). The Holy Fathers suggest the means to approach the Divine darkness, the hidden unknown.

The patristic tradition distinguishes two possible types of knowledge of God: the rational, cataphatic type and the ineffable, apophatic one. The latter is superior to the former and completes it. Belief goes further than reason. We can figure God cataphatically as the Wisdom and Force who created the world and sustains it, but apophatically we can have a "direct experience of His mystical presence." This presence of God transcends everything that is definable in words (Staniloae, 1998).

Philip told Jesus, *"Lord, show us the Father, and it is sufficient for us."* And Our Lord Jesus Christ replied, *"He who has seen Me has seen the Father"* (*John 14:8-9*). Fortunately, willing or not willing, knowing or ignoring, Christ is always next to us. As Father Lev Gillet says, the unknown traveler on the road to Emmaus (*Luke 24:13-35*), the gardener in the vicinity of the tomb (*John 20:14-18*) and the stranger standing on the lake shore (*John 21:1-14*) continue to meet us, hidden in our quotidian life confirming the Son's presence in the human being (Un moine de l'Église d'Orient, 1963). We have to find Him and through Him, the whole Holy Trinity.

Yet, with our own powers, we cannot ascend to His heights and we cannot understand and be truly close to our Teacher, Master and Savior. The prayer does this job for us by working mysteriously in us. It is the apophatic aspect of knowledge "with regard to the supraessential being of God." As the Syriac Father Mar Jacob teaches, where it is dark even for the highest rank of angels, man's prayer can find light: "The seraph hides its face from Divine Being with its wings, but prayer stands there unveiled before the Majesty" (quoted by Coniaris, 1998). The Finnish Orthodox writer Tito Colliander wrote, "Prayer is action; to pray is to be highly effective" (Colliander, 1985). As Saint Dyonisius the Areopagite wrote in his work *The Divine Names*, prayer might achieve the state necessary to know God which is "a total remove from every condition, movement, life, imagination, conjecture, name, discourse, thought, conception, being, rest, dwelling, unity, limit, infinity, [and] totality of existence" (quoted by Staniloae, 1998). "Without prayer there is no life. Prayer is our nature," wrote Father Kallistos (see Kallistos, 1989).

We have to listen to Christ and follow God's instructions which protect us from damaging our souls. *"You are My friends if you do whatever I command you,"* Jesus told His disciples. *"No longer do I call you servants, for a servant does not know what his master is doing; but I have called you friends, for all things that I heard from My Father I have made known to you"* (*John 15: 14-15*). Our daily life must flow in harmony with God's will because, as the Holy Fathers teach, God's way is not man's way even if sometimes they intersect or overlap. We have to understand that, and with the Lord in mind and heart, we have to take every unexpected thing with calm and to try to solve any new problem, trusting God's will and wisdom in everything.

Father Oleska, a priest in wild and beautiful Alaska, a continuously surprising state, describes this feeling with peaceful heart and much humor. "Alaska teaches a person to go with the flow. You may have plans, but a hundred unforeseen forces can join to overthrow them. You want to travel, but it's too foggy, too windy, too cold, too rainy, [or] too cloudy; the ice is too thin, the mud is too soft; the engine is broken, someone else is using it, no one cleaned it [or] prepared it. You're expecting a package, but the planes are not flying, the postmaster is sick, there is a funeral today, the plane couldn't bring the mail because there were too many boxes [or] too many people [and there's] not enough room in the cargo bay, the pilot forgot it, a sled dog ate it. Burger King advertises, "Have it your way!" Alaska warns, "Don't bet on it!" (Oleska, 2018). "*L'homme propose, Dieu dispose*," the old French people say (man suggests, Lord decides).

The Sixth Sunday after Pascha in the Orthodox Church and the Easter Tuesday in the Catholic Church, congregations hear a reading about Paul and Silas from the Book of Acts. Saint Paul expelled the evil spirit from the female slave who predicted future. Angry for losing his profit source the owner convinced the authorities to strip and beat Paul and Silas with rods, and to throw them in jail. By God's will, a strong earthquake shook the prison and all the gates opened. The frightened jailer had thus the revelation of God's power and asked for his and his entire family's baptism right away (see *Acts 16:16-34*). What is remarkable here, besides all the details, is the fact that, despite the harsh and bloody treatment the authorities subjected Paul and Silas to, both "*were praying and singing hymns to God*" instead of bitterly reproaching God for the injustice done to them. God answered the prayers and songs to their and others' benefits, and they accomplished their mission. Saint Augustine said, "Pray as if everything depends on God. Work as if everything depends on you." Saint Theophan the

Recluse warned us, "Prayer is the test of everything. If prayer is right, everything is right. Prayer is the root of all" (see Coniaris, 1998). In a bitter, apparently unjust case like that of the imprisoned missionaries, we might utter the David's humble words mentioned in an ode of ascents, *"O Lord, My heart is not exalted, neither are my eyes raised up, neither am I carried along in great things, nor in things too marvelous for me. If I were not humble-minded, but exalted my soul, like a child weaned from his mother, so You would reward my soul"* (*Psalm 130/131:1-2*).

Our salvation does not come instantly by confessing our faith in Jesus Christ as some Protestants believe. It is the combined result of our spiritual work and the grace of God; we are *regenerated* (reborn) at baptism, *justified* (acceptable to God) and *sanctified* (freed from sin) through our soul's process of deification. God involves us in His work for the salvation of humankind, always with the participation of our free will, as the Holy Virgin Mary said, *"Let it be to me according to your word"* (*Luke 1:38*). Father Coniaris (Coniaris, 1998) mentioned that Our Lord Jesus Christ "borrowed" from men a manger at his birth (*Luke 2:7*), a boat for preaching (*Luke 5:3*), loaves and fish to feed the crowds (*Luke 9:16*), a colt for entering Jerusalem on Palm Sunday (*Matthew 21:2-3*), a sponge on cross for His thirst (*Matthew 27:48*), and a spear for spilling His blood (*John 19:34*). This says much about Our Lord Jesus Christ's invitation for participation in His work of saving our souls.

Saint Gregory of Sinai advises, *"Cleanse your heart of passions and the predispositions of sin. How? Through inner attention and the return of the mind into the heart. Then practice sacred mental prayer in the heart, saying, 'Lord Jesus Christ, Son of God, have mercy upon me'"* (see Belonick, 1998). This advice reminds us Saint Apostle Paul's words who exhorts us to cleanse the filthiness, *"perfecting holiness <u>in the fear of God,</u>"* (*2 Corinthians 7:1*). Saint Paul added, *"Work out your own salvation with <u>fear and trembling</u>"* (*Philippians 2:12*). The fear of God is the beginning of wisdom. It is expressed in the obedience to the Lord, in the trust in Him and in the vigil not to lose the trail leading us straight to Him. If we do so, the benefit would be great (*Psalm 18/19*). *"The fear of the Lord increases days, but the years of the ungodly will be shortened"* (*Proverbs 10:28*). Indeed, the real length of our life is, as Saint Paisius of Neamts noted, <u>the very period we are with Him</u>. Life can be rich even if its number of years might be short in calendar. By persevering in our work of purification and growth of virtue, the fear which opened the gate will be replaced by the love of truth which will lead us towards the Lord, because that love is the love of a really beneficent life, the Love for God who is our parent who created us and cares for us. Then, understanding the real essence of our existence and the beauty of the universe in which the Lord positioned us, we will say together with the Apostle, *"God has not given us a spirit of fear, but of power and of love and of a sound mind"* (*2 Timothy 1:7*).

   Fear of God and trust in Him help us in our battle for growing virtues and defeating the passions, and the Jesus Prayer is a strong weapon in our unseen war. Saint Thalassios the Libyan in his writing "On Love, Self-Control and Life in Accordance with the

Intellect," named the steps necessary in the process of cleansing our soul: "The first renunciation is that of material things, the second that of the passions, the third that of ignorance." And regarding the latter, which refers to the conscious control of our mind, he noted, "There are three ways through which thoughts arise in you: through the senses, through the memory, and through the body's temperament. Of these the most irksome are those that come through the memory" (see *The Philokalia*, 1981).

We learn from Saint Maximos the Confessor's writing *Four Hundred Texts on Love*: "There are said to be five reasons why God allows us to be assailed by demons. The first is so that, by attacking and counterattacking, we should learn to discriminate between virtues and vice. The second is so that, having acquired virtue through conflict and toil, we should keep it secure and immutable. The third is so that, when making progress in virtue, we should not become haughty but learn humility. The fourth is so that, having gained some experience of evil, we should '*hate it with perfect hatred*' (cf. *Psalm 138/139:22*). The fifth and most important is so that, having achieved dispassion, we should forget neither our own weakness nor the power of Him who has helped us" (see *The Philokalia*, 1981). The fight against the temptations the evil spirit launches against us does not cease until the end of our earthly life but we should never give up; prayer is our weapon and through it the Lord strengthens us. "Since passions are tamed by prayer, when they arise, we should practice the Jesus Prayer inwardly, very quietly and without haste," Saint Ignatius Brianchaninov wrote (see Belonick, 1998).

According to the saintly Abbot Isaiah, "Jesus Prayer is a mirror for the mind and a lantern for the conscience" (quoted by Colliander, 1985). Our heart is like a house targetted by thieves who are "the evil impulses." Jesus Prayer is the warning voice of the guard who watches, and, to our great good, the person who keeps watch is not us anymore but Christ Himself (see Colliander, 1985). The prayer is deep in the heart and even if the mind is absent, distracted or tired, the heart watches: "*I sleep, but my heart keeps watch*" (*Song of Songs 5:2*). Saint Mark the Monk said that "the rational mind cannot rest idle for thoughts keep filling it with ceaseless chatter" (see Kallistos, 1986).

The deep wisdom of the Philokalia reminds us that we have to do our work and then, without pride but with humility and trust in the Lord, ask for His grace which makes our striving really fruitful: "When we have attained some degree of holiness we should always repeat to ourselves the words of the Apostle: '*Yet not I, but the grace of God which was with me*' (*1 Corinthians 15:10*), as well as what was said by the Lord [Jesus Christ]: '*Without Me you can do nothing*' (*John 15:5*). We should also bear in mind what the prophet said: '*Unless the Lord builds the house, they labor in vain that build it*' (*Psalm 126/127:1*), and finally: '*It does not depend on man's will or effort, but on God's mercy*' (*Romans 9:16*)... The Apostle Paul asks: "*What do you have which you did not receive? Now if you received it, why do you boast, as if you had not received it?*' (*1 Corinthians 4:7*). What right, then, has man to be proud as though he could achieve perfection through his own efforts?" (see Saint John Cassian's writing in *The Philokalia*, 1982).

"*Christ* [embodies among us] *the power of God and the wisdom of God*" (*1 Corinthians 1:24*). He is Messiah, Jesus Christ, the Son of God incarnated in "a rod from the root of Jesse," and a flower "of his root" (Coniaris, 1998). It is He we should address first. Through Him we can access the whole Holy Trinity. By uniting us to Christ, the son of God, through the Jesus Prayer, we are able to address the whole Holy Trinity due to its unit in three hypostases (*Perichoresis*).

Our Lord Jesus Christ told His disciples (and we, all the Christians, can consider ourselves also His disciples), "*Most assuredly, I say to you, whatever you ask the Father in My name He will give you*" (*John 16:23*). "*For there is one God and one Mediator between God and men, the Man Christ Jesus*," the Apostle Saint Paul wrote to his favorite spiritual son (*1 Timothy 2:5*). Father Lev Gillet, signing sometimes with much humility "Un Moine de l'Église d'Orient" (A Monk of the Eastern Church), remarked that actually the core (the heart) of the Gospel is Jesus Christ and more specifically the mystery of the relationship between God the Father and His unique Son. And Pope John Paul II correctly said that the Divine Liturgy is in fact a prayer of Jesus Christ to God the Father.

We know and follow God the Father through His Son who deified our humanity by the incarnation of Jesus Christ. Saint Paul advises us, "*Whatever you do in word or deed, do all in the name of the Lord Jesus, giving thanks to God the Father through Him*" (*Colossians 3:17*). This way we will have the chance to reach Saint Paul's holiness who firmly affirmed, "*It *is no longer I who live, but Christ lives in me*" (*Galatians 2:20*).

Christ's missionary work was continued in our world by the Holy Spirit through whom the Lord acts in us. He told the disciples, "*If I do not go away, the Helper will not come to you*" (*John 16:7*). The Helper is "*the Holy Spirit, whom the Father will send in My name, He will teach you all things and bring to your remembrance all things that I said to you,*" as Christ indicated (*John 14:26*). Consequently, now when we address Jesus, the Son of God, our prayers, thoughts and feelings go in fact through the Holy Spirit, due to the indestructible, mysterious unit of the Holy Trinity. "*The Spirit of God shall rest upon Him, the Spirit of wisdom and understanding, the Spirit of counsel and might, the Spirit of knowledge and godliness, the Spirit of the fear of God shall fill Him*" (*Isaiah 11:1-3*). Our work as Christ's apprentices will attract therefore the Holy Spirit's perfecting travail on our soul and being, and He will enrich us with the Holy Spirit's gifts: "*The fruit of the Spirit is love, joy, peace, longsuffering, kindness, goodness, faithfulness, gentleness, self-control*" (*Galatians 5:22-23*).

In conclusion, we address the Godhead – Father, Son and Holy Spirit - through the Divine Person who is the closest to our condition: Jesus Christ Who deified our human nature by the incarnation of God the Son Who remained at the same time in His high place. "Wholly present was the infinite Word among those below, yet in no way absent from those on high; for this was a divine condescension and not a change of place" (Eikos 8 in *Akathistos to Theotokos*). His name, the only actual accessible part of the Godhead's name, opens the gate for our soul's entrance into the spiritual heights that our whole being needs so much. Christ Himself emphasized the Power of Name – a power which frightens men by its enormous size but comforts them by its beneficient and loving action. He did that when He prayed to God the Father in reference to the disciples before His Passion: *"Holy Father, keep through <u>Your Name</u> those whom You have given Me ... as You, Father, are in Me, and I in You; that they also may be one in Us"* (*John 17:11* and *21*). God the Father's name (I AM, *Exodus 3:14*), that His Son bears (*John 4:26*; *8:58*; *13:19*) is frightening: when God the Son incarnate, Jesus, said "*I am*" the armed soldiers who came to arrest him fell to the ground, frightened to death (*John 18:6*). Therefore, we use Jesus' name in our prayers and not the other name that only He can use.

Father Lev Gillet wrote that when we pronounce Jesus' name, we pronounce the word who was "*in the beginning*" (*John 1:1*), the Word that God the Father pronounces from His eternity. "Pronouncing Jesus' name means approaching God the Father, contemplating the love and gift of the Fathers focusing on Jesus" (see Un moine de l'Église d'Orient, 1963). It is the love Christ referred to, in His prayer, and which is transferred to the disciples: *"the love with which You loved Me may be in them, and I in them"* (*John 17:26*).

The name's power results from its intimate relationship with the soul. The name we receive at baptism and the name the monks receive at ordination establish a God-blessed strong and tight connection with the soul. Let us think that when the chosen people made an important spiritual progress, the Lord marked that with a name change. Thus, He changed the name

Abram into Abraham (*Genesis 17:5*), the name Jacob into Israel (*Genesis 32:28*), the name Saul into Paul (*Acts 13:9*). The Lord might identify each of us with a secret name known only by Him in addition to our ordinary name. Father Kalistos commented that to know somebody's name is often "to gain an insight into his nature and thereby to acquire a relationship with him" and even "a certain control over him.". This is why the angel who fought with Jacob (Genesis 32:29) and the angel who talked with Manoah (Judge 13:18) refused to say their name (Kallistos, 1986); their names were known only by the Master of the Universe.

"Lord Jesus Christ, Son of God, have mercy on me, a sinner." The power of the name present in the Jesus Prayer derives actually from four appelatives. The first is "Lord"; "we recognize the Lordship of Christ, enthrone Him in our life," in our mind for thinking, in our heart for purity, in our will for faith. The second is "Jesus" which is "the human name of God." The third is "Christ" which "is the fulfillment of the Old Testament." The fourth is "Son of God" because He is "truly the Only Begotten Son."

The words "have mercy" do not mean the simple fact that we are weak and ask for forgiveness, but that we need a favorable response to our "longing for reconciliation" because "we are aware that our vocation is great and our power is weak." The word "sinner" shows that we have broken "the Law of God," and because of that we have damaged our "contact with God, with our own conscience, with our own life, and with our neighbor's life" (Bloom, 1989). Father Ambrose of Optina (see above the chapter about the

Elders of Optina) was asked if one should place the emphasis on the word "Jesus." He replied that it is better to emphasize the word "sinner."

Saint Seraphim of Sarov suggested a longer formula of Jesus Prayer: "Lord Jesus Christ, Son of God, by the prayers of the Mother of God, have mercy on me a sinner" (see *Little Russian Philokalia, vol. I,* 1980). This implies that the Theotokos is the best intercessory for us, before all the other Saints, because only her humanity, the purest of all, could shelter the Divine Jesus and because, through the Savior's words said on the cross, she is a Mother for the whole believing humankind (see *John 19:26-27*).

Practicing the Jesus Prayer is not in fact developing a prayer tool inside ourselves but "an attentive, respectful, reverent, worshipful awareness" that we can use any moment in our dialogue with God (see Bloom, 1989). In addition to that, Saint Teophane the Recluse teaches, "Simply enter into every word and then bring the meaning of each word down into your heart. That is, understand what you say, and then experience what you have understood" (see Belonick, 1998). Metropolitan Anthony Bloom points out the fact that in all Orthodox icons Mother of God is not depicted looking toward her Divine son or to us or into the distance but inside herself – "she is in contemplation" (Bloom, 1970). Thus, we should be focused while praying. We need stillness, as a little hesychia, for mental quietude in order to hear God and to open our heart to Him. Eventually the silence becomes a presence. "At the heart of the silence there is Him who is all stillness, all peace, all poise," said the French writer Georges Bernanos (quoted by Bloom, 1970).

In order to more easily focus our attention on the sacred things, Saint Seraphim of Sarov indicated that when we are attending the Church service we should "stand with closed eyes in internal mindfulness," deepened into the prayer of praise, thanks and request in which the Divine Liturgy is, having in its core Jesus Christ's sacrifice, the Eucharist. In case our mind gets trapped in distractions coming from outside and its thoughts run away we should humble ourselves and say, "I have sinned, Lord, by word, deed, thought, and by all my feelings." And if we are tired and tend to doze "we should fix our eyes upon an icon and the candle burning before it" (see Little Russian Philokalia, vol. I, 1980).

Prayer disciplines our spirit. If our prayer is not answered is because the prayer first has to be conducive to the salvation of our soul and only after that for fulfilling our material needs. <u>Seek God first</u> before speaking about both our own and our neighbor's needs. Father Staniloae commented, "In my relation to God, of course, my prayer is not reciprocated – God does not pray to man, man prays to God. There is, however, mutual giving. Man realizes his freedom not only by receiving it from God through prayer but also by giving himself to God. Only so does man gain freedom from himself. If he tries to hold on to the existence he has received from God in love, he loses his freedom; wanting to be arbiter of his own existence he becomes its slave… He can only be free if he <u>lives for God and in God</u>" (Staniloae, 1996).

Our repentance is a very important factor for being heard in our petitions but also for our spiritual ascent. "Repentance is a forum superior to man, always raising him above the moral and spiritual levels which he has reached." It fills us with uneasiness, with unhealed and ceaseless pressure. Our toils and snares are purposely allowed to happen. "Let all involuntary suffering teach you to remember God, and you will not lack occasion for repentance," the Holy Fathers teach us (see St. Mark the Ascetic, "On the Spiritual Law: Two Hundred Texts" No. 57 in *The Philokalia*, 1982). Repentance awakens us and it is "sustained by the intuition of an authority higher than us, to whom we feel responsible, but which also gives us power to do more, if we ask Him for it" (Staniloae, 2002). Repentance is saluted by Heavens in gladness. Our Lord Jesus said, *"I tell you, there is joy before the angels of God over one sinner who repents"* (*Luke 15:10*).

We should not forget Jesus' words, *"You are my friends if you do whatever I command you. No longer do I call you servant... but I have called you friends"* (*John 15:14-15*). He also said, *"I chose you and appointed you that you should go and bear fruit and that fruit should remain, that whatever you ask the Father in My name He may give you"* (*John 15:16*). Therefore, a Jesus Prayer bearer is similar to the converted Saul (Saint Paul), whom Jesus, in His conversation with Ananias called *"a chosen vessel of Mine to bear My name"* (*Acts 9:15*).

The best indication that we are closer to the end of our road of deification is the stage of true love dwelling in our soul – the Love for God and the love for neighbors as the Gospel summarized the ten commandments (*Matthew 22:37-40, Mark 12:29-31, and Luke 10:27-28*). Only then we will be able to respond to the Lord's call, *"You shall eat and drink at the table of My Kingdom*" (*Luke 22:30*). Saint Isaac the Syrian noted, "When we have reached love, we have reached God and our way is ended" (quoted by Kallistos, 1986). This is another aspect achieved by Jesus Prayer, as a tool in our continuous striving toward spiritual improvement on our way to deification: answering the Second Commandment of our Savior which is the love for our neighbor. Saint Seraphim of Sarov's words are inspiring: "Acquire inner peace and thousands around you will find their salvation." By working for God in stable faith we achieve the peace of our soul which transfigures our relationship with the others and it grows into love. "The Jesus Prayer makes each into a 'man for others,' a living instrument of God's peace, a dynamic center of reconciliation" (Kallistos, 1986).

A Philokalic Holy Father wrote, "Just as the thought of fire does not warm the body, so faith without love does not actualize the light of spiritual knowledge in the soul" (Saint Maximos the Confessor in Four Hundred Texts on Love 1.31-32 – *The Philokalia*, 1981). Another one commented, "Blessed is the monk who considers all humans like God after God. Blessed is the monk who enjoys like his precious assets the accomplishment of salvation by others and the spiritual progress of all. This is the monk who, by isolating himself from the all others, becomes united with them" (see Saint Evagrius Ponticus, named also the Solitary, quoted by Clément, 1977). The same Saint also said, "When does a man know that his heart achieved purity? When he considers all humans good, without thinking that some are impure or soiled. Then truly his heart is pure" (Clément, 1977).

We can say the Jesus Prayer as an intercessory prayer, by simply looking at a person or thinking of him/her, and by slightly modifying the prayer formula to: "Lord Jesus Christ, Son of God, have mercy on us" or "... have mercy on him/her." Bishop Mark of Ladoga remembered the outstanding power of the Jesus Prayer experienced during his teenage novitiate at Valaam Monastery in Russia (see Stakhovich, 1995). He was quite intrigued by an enigmatic monk whom the others called Michael the Silent because when Michael had entered the community, he had made the promise not to talk at all. In his humble obedience, he worked in the kitchen, in the steam of the boiling food, and was always dirty with soot and grease. He never participated in the church services, preferring the solitude he found in the kitchen, the noisiest place in the monastery. The young novice watched him often with curiosity but Brother Michael never paid attention, focused on his pots and spoons, always looking down deepened in great silence. One day the youth dashed to the kitchen and surprised Brother Michael who, being alone, stood in the middle of the room with raised arms, weeping bitterly with tears flowing down his face. Not seeing the intruder, the old man was crying loudly in a foreign language imploring God's mercy and forgiveness. The youth understood that this man, in his non-talking solitude, was a Jesus Prayer bearer.

The novice was very much loved by the Abbot and the others who saw in him a promising future Elder. Unfortunately, it happened that, to their deep worry and sorrow, the novice fell sick and the doctor said that he would soon die. The Abbot Harriton would have wished to give his own life in turn for the life of his spiritual son. On Good Saturday somebody suggested to tonsure him on his deathbed in order to give him the chance to repose the next day on the Great Feast of Easter and thus to be received by the Lord as a monk. The novice accepted and immediately became unconscious. In great haste the old Abbot and the other brought the monk clothes, said the service and changed his lay name from Leonid to his monk's name Mark because it was Saint Evangelist Mark's Day. After finishing all the service prayers and rules, the miracle occurred: the moribund man opened his eyes and with effort rose up. The next day, although still very weak, he was present at the Divine Liturgy, sharing with the others the unique great joy of the Holy Resurrection of Christ.

For unknown reasons the convalescent monk Mark thought often of Brother Michael. A long time later, while in the kitchen he told the others about the miracle of his healing, how he actually was resurrected on Good Saturday, on Saint Mark's Day. Suddenly Mark noticed that Brother Michael in his quiet corner stopped his work, turned toward the wall to hide his face, kept his back bent while he held a big pot of grease in his hands, and listened intently to the youth's story. After Mark finished his enthusiastic story, all the people left and the kitchen was covered by deep silence. Remained alone, Mark watched Brother Michael closely and tried to guess why the latter was so interested in his story. After a long break, thinking that the room is empty, Brother Michael slowly turned back from the wall with a light coughing. He stretched his back and raised his forehead. His lips moved in a barely visible smile under the tears staining his face.

His eyes, wide open, were full of light (were they blue or gray?). The young monk realized immediately that the prayers of that very humble brother, maybe a Saint, were those which caused the Lord's answer in his miraculous healing. Behold, someone hidden in the steam and soot of the kitchen, among the big, dirty pots, knew what was going on in the monastery and was praying with deep love and tears for the others! Mark's knees melted, his body was penetrated by an unearthly light and in the very bottom of his heart he heard very clearly what his ears did not hear – Brother Michael's inner voice saying, "Yes, my dear, that was I, because I love you." However, that last only a few seconds because the older man bowed his head, looked down again, and with his back bent he resumed scraping the big greasy pot.

Many years passed by and monk Mark was recruited into WWII. After the war was over and he returned to Valaam, nobody remembered anything else about the old Brother Michael than that he died one unknown day... Today Brother Michael is enlisted in the Valaam Patericon and is commemorated on September 6 (he reposed in 1939).

Some readers might wonder about the real benefit of all these things for us who are not isolated in a remote monastic environment but who are living in the midst of the crowds, exposed to all the aspects of the society. First of all we can find an answer in Saint John Climacus' advices for the laity mentioned above in the Foreword section. We also have the words of the great Russian Theologian from France, Paul Evdokimov, that all God believers are a sort of monks in the depth of their soul and a sort of hermits in the outside, earthly world. Our Lord Jesus Christ said about His disciples in His prayer to God the Father, "*They are not of the world, just as I am not of the world*" (*John 17:16*).

One can see a secret symbol above the entrance door into the church of Antim Monastery in Bucharest: a snail carrying his shell-house climbs slowly but sure to the heights. Monks or laymen, we carry with us, everywhere we go, our hidden shut-door room of prayer (*Matthew 6:6*), as the snail does with its shell. The place where our heart thinks of God is there, in our deep inner side; this is also the place where the diligent, zealous people breathe the Jesus Prayer. Our Lord Jesus Christ, who took a human body, a body made in God's image and according to His likeness (see *Genesis 1:26*), abides in that protected inner space, in the intimacy of our soul. "*It is no longer I who live, but Christ lives in me*," Saint Paul said (*Galatians 2:20*). From that secret place Christ understands us, teaches us, leads us and listens to the whisper of our prayer.

Not sharing the society's superficiality, rubbles and tinsels does not mean that we hate the world. On the contrary we end by loving its essence – the presence of God Which is hidden in all that is good in each person. The priest Kenneth Leech was right when he wrote in his Introduction to Collinder's book, "The material world is the vehicle, nor the enemy, of the spirit. All spirituality has a material basis." As Saint John Damascene pointed out, "the Creator 'became material' and through matter effected our salvation" (see Colliander, 1985). Therefore, returning to the matter of our existence in the midst of the society, Jesus Prayer is not only for monks and nuns but also for the whole laity, as very correctly Father Kallistos noted – for married people, doctors, psychiatrists, social workers or bus drivers (Kallistos, 1986).

Father Arseny Streltzoff was a Russian priest-monk, previously an art historian, who spent 26 years in the Soviet Goulag, in the period 1933-1958. Although not canonized he was a real Saint and was very much beloved. After his death in 1973 stories from his life were collected from people who knew him and the resulted book became very popular despite the fact that it was passed around secretly, as a samizdat, punishable by the atheist communist government. Father Arseny was a man of ardent prayer and a Jesus Prayer bearer. "While he was doing his [detention hard] work he prayed the akathist, his rule of prayer, vespers, matins, and all the other prayers a priest must pray." Very often, inprisoned in Siberian extermination camps together with thieves and murderers, under very inhumane conditions, he spent the whole night praying and despite the hunger, cold and exhaustion from labor in the woods, he felt refreshed in the morning.

Humble and full of love for the others he took care of the sick. One of them was Ivan Sazikov, an infamous criminal, guilty of armed robbery, beating and murder. He noticed Father Arseny's lips moving, while Father was helping him, and exploded sarcastically, "You are praying, eh, priest?! You pray to get forgiveness of your sins and this is why you help us! You're afraid of God! Why's that? Have you ever seen Him?" Father replied that sure enough he feels God's presence uniting their souls although Sazikov's soul was black with heavy sins. To Sazikov's great surprise, Father addressed him with his baptism name Seraphim, a name which was not in the official documents and nobody knew. With a gentle voice Father ensured the prisoner that "Saint Seraphim of Sarov will not abandon" him. This made Sazikov even mad and with disfigured face yelled at him full of hatred, "I'll kill you, silly priest, I'll kill you. I don't know how you know things. I hate the way you think." Father, in silence, reacted inside with the prayer flow, "have mercy on me, a sinner," and continued to take tender care of him. Later, after a long process in the depth of his soul, Sazikov became a believer, asked for confession, and remained very attached to the humbled priest even after being freed from prison (see *Father Arseny*... 2001).

The prayer life of Father Arseny is a good example of combining prayer in solitude, remote from any source of distraction, with the prayer in the midst of multitude. The Holy Fathers say that the evening (night) prayer is gold, the morning prayer is silver, the midday prayer is brass; the first two are done in solitude, when we are alone with God, chasing away all thoughts of other things, the latter is done during our activities when God transparency comes through our neighbors and the nature, transfiguring them.

An important part of the Jesus Prayer's power derives from its constant repetition. The repetition makes mind and heart become more familiar with prayers in general and with this Prayer in particular. By repeating this prayer, we can apply its wisdom and emotion to each moment and space of our continuously varying daily existence. All thoughts and feelings, which run back and forth escaping from our control, gain the chance to be exposed to the Jesus Prayer that is said at that very moment and thus receive its inspiring treasury of answers. Eventually, as Father Kallistos observed, the repetitive aspect of the Jesus Prayer causes the transfiguration of our relationship with the creation around us and with other humans. It makes all things "transparent, changing them into a sacrament of God's presence" on one hand and it "helps us to see Christ in each" of our neighbors on the other hand (Kallistos, 1986). As a result, the Invocation of the Divine Name in the Jesus Prayer fills our soul with a joyful and not "penitential" sound, with a "world-affirming" feeling "rather than world-denying," and becomes a source "of liberation and healing" instead of being "somber and oppressive" (Kallistos, 1986). Father Kallistos emphasized a general principle for any prayer but especially important here at saying the Jesus Prayer. "As we invoke the Name, we should not deliberately shape in our minds any visual image of the Savior", he said, quoting also Saint Gregory of Sinai's advice to keep the intellect "free from colors, images and forms" (Kallistos, 1986).

The young brethren asked Abba Agathon, an Egyptian Saint contemporary to Saint Makarios the Great, what virtue requires the greatest effort. The long-experienced Abba replied, "Forgive me, but I think that there is no labor greater than praying to God. Every time a man wants to pray, his enemies try to prevent him... In everything else that man undertakes if he perseveres, he will attain rest. But in order to pray, a man must struggle to his last breath" (see Coniaris, 1998). The Jesus Prayer has the attributes of a reliable, companionable prayer, a friendly one, always at hand

and very personal in spite of its monotonous repetitions. We should not worry that this Prayer might be ineffective due to its very simple, few and unvarying words; it "reaches out beyond words into the living silence of the Eternal" (Kallistos, 1986). This Prayer is, as Father Kallistos wrote, a kind of "arrow prayer", which is short, with "fervent invocations frequently repeated" (Coniaris, 1998). Whether in joy or in sorrow, this Prayer makes, when it becomes habitual, a quickening of the soul ready to respond to any call of God. Thus, we will reach the situation Saint Symeon, the New Theologian, was referring to when he advised, "Do not worry about what will come next, you will discover it when it comes" (see Bloom, 1966).

A Polish writer commented, "Although the Jesus Prayer belongs to the Orthodox tradition, something akin to it was also proposed in other traditions. A protestant author wrote that many a dear mother of mediocre ability, walking through life, whispering 'Jesus' every moment will do more to sweeten and save humanity than all the cunning schemes of diplomats" (Drozdek, 2014).

"The Jesus Prayer is not a device to help us concentrate or relax. It is not simply a piece of 'Christian Yoga', a type of 'Transcendental Meditation', or a 'Christian mantra'... It is, on contrary, an invocation specifically addressed to another person – to God made man, Jesus Christ, our personal Savior and Redeemer," Father Kallistos wrote (Kallistos, 1986). Some authors (like Clément, 1977) noticed similarities between the body techniques practiced by the Hesychasts, Hindu Yogis (*japa-yoga*), Japanese (*nembutsu*), and Islamic Sufis (*dhikr*), but these physical, mainly breathing, procedures which have to be carefully supervised by an experienced spiritual instructor, are actually secondary for the regular laypeople as Saint Gregory of Palamas (1296-1359) emphasized. Our primary concern should be directing our attention to the Name invocated, to Our Lord Jesus Christ. This is also the philosophy of the well-known booklet "The Way of a Pilgrim" promoted by the Optina Elders, which spread so widely throughout Orthodox Christianity. It seems that the hero of that journey's booklet, in search of the key to an unceasing prayer, succeeded in saying the Jesus Prayer 12,000 times a day without effort (see Coniaris 1998), which means about 12 sayings per minute! Father Kallistos quoted Saint Ignatius Brianchaninov's advice for us, permanently beginners, living a social life and not a monastic or hermitic one: "the breathing technique is fully replaced by the unhurried enunciation of the Prayer, by a short rest or pause at the end, each time it is said, by gentle and unhurried [normal] breathing, and by the enclosure of the mind in the words of the Prayer."

In order to have an indication about the speed of saying it, we can remember that for a hundred Jesus Prayers we should need half an hour (see Kallistos, 1986). People sometimes use prayer-ropes with a hundred knots for keeping track of the repetitions. However, for beginners, quantitative measurements are not important.

We have not to forget another major thing: because of the weakness of the spirit of the beginners of all levels as we are, Jesus Prayer cannot become an *unceasing* prayer in Saint Paul's terms, blent into our breath as long as our body is alive. Therefore, it is very important that, besides practicing Jesus Prayer, we continue to say all the other prayers that Church teaches us to say. People who are less diligent, with a less stringent and burning call, who do not have a special time of the day dedicated to the practice of multiple sayings, may opt for a simple use of the Jesus Prayer on every occasion of the day: waking up, before and after meals, before starting work, in moments of high emotion, of fear, of incertitude, of danger, of much joy, of love for others, of peace. We can say it also in many other circumstances as for instance when somebody bothers us, when we lose control of our feelings, or when we bless somebody in our mind. Metropolitan Anthony has a suggestion for people who are very busy the whole day and not able to dedicate hours to God. "We can easily single out one or two moments [in the day] and put all our energy into them... If we try to pray continuously, we will be defeated quite soon; but if we choose moments intelligently, we can do it," Metropolitan Anthony wrote (Bloom, 1970).

Often when we drive on a familiar road, when we are caught in a traffic jam, when we perform a semi-mechanical work that does not require much mental effort, when we dig in the garden, when we do a puzzle or crosswords, when we rest our tired body in an armchair or when walk in the nature for relaxation after a busy day, we feel the need of music in background and we resort to our iPod and headphones. The airports and the medical offices know this thing and offer a musical background to the waiting people. The shopkeepers use it in a more cunning way by inducing our mind's exigent discernment to somnolence while we do our shopping. The modern world is very sophisticated and invites us to buy CD's with stimulating music for the beginning of our day and for breakfast, dreaming music when we supper in a restaurant, soothing music before going to bed. We also can play sounds recorded from the nature as the sunny-day birds' chirping at breakfast, the monotonous and repetitive sound of the sea waves or of the wind in the leaves at sleeping time. All of these can be replaced very well with the intimate Jesus Prayer or with just the thought to Jesus and Mother of God. Our heart will find in them what she needs and what she is longing for: quietness, encouragement, inspiration, gaiety, light humor, energy.

We pray first fearing the work of evil, but later when God gives us His peace, we pray fearing not to lose that peace. Unfortunately, "we are only dimly aware of our need for prayer." To make things worse, prayer seems often to be pretty difficult, uncomfortable and tiresome but this is because "we fail to make it a part of our own experience," of our daily existence (Bloom, 1989).

We can mark all the 24 hours of the day with our Jesus Prayer and thoughts sent to the Lord. At 6 a.m. we thank God for the light of the sun which starts the working day and ask that the light of Christ on Mount Tabor transfigure us. At 9 a.m. we remember that it is the hour of the Pentecost and we pray through Our Lord Jesus to the Holy Spirit to descend and bless our day. At 12 p.m. we think of Christ crucified and we thank Him for His love and for choosing to suffer for our good. At 3 p.m. we remember His death on the cross and ask Him to receive us like the penitent thief in the heavens when the time of our repose will come.

At sunset, at 6 p.m., we welcome Christ, the True Light, and ask that the rest of the day as the remainder of our life may pass in peace and without sin; "O Gladsome Light of the holy glory of the Immortal Father, heavenly, holy, blessed Jesus Christ. Now we have come to the setting of the sun and behold the light of the evening," the choir sings in church at Vespers; we are aware that the cycle of the Creation Day actually commences at the sunset not at sunrise – "and there was evening and morning, one day" (Genesis 1.5). At 9 p.m., we can think of the darkness of sin and death that covered the world after Christ died on cross and we can pray to Him to pull us out from the dark and stinking swamp to Him Who is the true Light of the universe. At midnight, "the entire creation rests for a moment in order to praise the Lord: the stars, the trees, the waters stop for a short space of time, and the whole army of angels who serve praise God at that hour along with the souls of righteous," Hippolytus explained in his writing *Apostolic Tradition*; we praise God and watch for the Savior's coming – "Behold, a cry is heard in the middle of the night of one saying, 'Behold the bridegroom is coming.'" At 3 a.m., when the cockcrow rises up we can pray again, repenting, because it is the hour when "the children of Israel denied Christ" (see Coniaris, 1998 and *Praying with the Orthodox Tradition*, 1996b).

As we learn from the Holy Fathers, the Jesus Prayer might be a vocal prayer, said with participation but remaining still exterior to our soul (this is commonly our beginners' level), a mental prayer (the Prayer of the Mind, the prayer of the *nous*) or a heart prayer (the

Prayer of the Heart, when the intellect descends into the heart). The majority of us, the lay people, are in the first stage but that does not mean we should not try to go deeper and to elevate our prayer to the higher stages. "Just as the light of the sun attracts a healthy eye, so through love knowledge of God naturally draws to itself the pure intellect," Saint Maximos the Confessor wrote in his *Four Hundred Texts on Love*, words that might refer to the Prayer of the Mind (*The Philokalia*, 1981). The last kind of prayer, the Prayer of the Heart, is the supreme spiritual level, when the Prayer dwells so deep inside that even words are not spoken anymore; the Elders reach this stage but even they cannot stay too long in this state.

It is a state of infinite joy and peace, of full communication with God, when sometimes by the Lord's work, a transfiguring light covers the praying person; it is a state that one is extremely happy when is in it and full of regret when is back out. Saint Paul described it in his epistle to Corinthians (*2 Corinthians 12:1-10*). The taboric light, the fire of the prayer was depicted in "The Icon of Prayer" venerated by the Burning Bush Movement in Romania (1945-1958), as commented in a previous chapter.

A last comment though: The Jesus Prayer does not eliminate the practice of other prayers which have to go on. As Tito Colliander mentioned, only the angels in heaven can be facing God all the time (Matthew 18:10); we have "an earthly body with its own cravings" and, as beginners, are not able to be in an uninterrupted prayer like the angels in their continuous prayers of praise (see Colliander, 1985).

SAINT PAISIUS, PRAY FOR US. We are greatful to Saint Paisius for teaching us to pray. "Having become a stranger on earth, you reached the heavenly fatherland, O venerable Father Paisius. You instructed the faithful to lift up their minds to God, and to cry out to Him with all their hearts, 'O Lord Jesus Christ, Son of God, have mercy on me a sinner'" (Troparion, tone 2). He continues to be an intercessor for us in heaven. "O Paisius, the joy of Russia, the boast of Athos and the wonder of Moldavia, by thy Divinely-inspired teaching thou dost direct us to the fount of wisdom and salvation. And now, enjoying in heaven the vision of Christ God, entreat Him that He may grant us His great mercy and save our souls" (Troparion, tone 4).

We praise him for his monastic light with the words of the old Akathist from Neamts Monastery: "Most blessed Father, following Christ's call you left the house of your parents because you did not find rest in your motherland. You became a hermit at Mount Athos, you settled as a new Abraham on the blessed Romanian land, where you cared as a great Abbot and Father, with numerous spiritual sons in the Moldavian country. For that, piously we cry to you: Rejoice, devout Father Paisius, great adviser of monks!" (Kontakion 1 in *Viața și Acatistul Sfântului Cuvios Paisie de la Neamț*, 2012).

We pray him to protect us with his powerful prayers. "Help us, most blessed Father Paisius, to follow Christ's commandments, and pray, together with the heaven's inhabitants, for our hierarchs, priests and monks, for mothers and children, for those in need and suffering, for all the righteous Christians and for the peace of Christ's Church, that we should be protected from evil by the grace of the Holy Trinity, to whom praise and thanks are due for ever. Amen." (Prayer in *Viața și Acatistul Sfântului Cuvios Paisie de la Neamț*, 2012). The paisianic spiritual movement represented an authentic Christian Renaissance accomplished in the very century of Voltaire and the Enlightenment. It marked profoundly the monastic life in the Eastern Europe. Despite the fact that Saint Paisius was born in Ukraine, he tied together, with his life and work, three great spiritual sites of his century: the Russian monasteries Optina and Valaam, the Greek monasteries of Mount Athos and the Romanian monasteries of Walachia and Moldavia. Metropolitan Bloom correctly noticed that "every nationality, every ethnic group, has something to contribute to each other group in terms of the knowledge of God" (Bloom, 1989) and, I think, this makes the beauty and power of our Orthodox belief.

Due to the tradition built by him and by his disciples, Saint Paisius continues to be a bright presence not only in the Romanian and the Russian Orthodox autocephalies but also in the American one, through Saint Herman of Alaska who, besides Saint Innocent, is probably the greatest Saint of the New World's Orthodox community. Saint Herman of Alaska, who is also the Patron Saint of the Americas, came from Valaam Monastery and brought with him the book received from the Abbot Nazarius, called "Dobrotolublye" which was written by Saint Paisius, as a Slavonic translation of **The Philokalia**.

Saint Paisius is indeed a "sacred bridge to the Holy Fathers," as says a new Akathist, composed by two young monks from Monks' Lagoon, in Saint Herman's Spruce Island, in Alaska. "Champion amidst the Holy Fathers, who leadest us across the abyss of unbelief in this fallen world, as a bridge to the paternal embrace of the fathers of old. Weep not, O brethren, but rejoice for we have a sure leader. Rejoice, Blessed Paisius, sacred bridge to the Holy Fathers" (Akathist, Kontakion 1 in *The Bicentennial of St. Paisius Velichkovsky*, 1994b). His labor of love is our hope and our joy in Christ. "Although we have been deprived of beholding thy bright face and thy sweet words, we have as our only consolation in sorrows thy heavenly intercession and thine unending legacy which comes into our warm embrace. Holding steadfast to thy labor of love we cry unto God: Alleluia" (Akathist, Kontakion 12 in *The Bicentennial of St. Paisius Velichkovsky*, 1994b).

May the Jesus Prayer, said from the depth of our heart, protect us with the tremendous power of the Lord's Holy Name in our life journey. "Bless the Lord, o my soul! And all that is within me, <u>bless His Holy Name</u>. Blessed are Thou, O Lord!" (The First Antiphon of the Divine Liturgy).

✟

Bibliography

*** 1936: *Sbornik.* [Texts about the Jesus Prayer]. Sortavalassa Oy Raamattutalon kirjapainossa. Valaam Monastery, Karelia (in Finland at that time). Translated in Romanian in 1945-1946 and spread under communism, in samizdat, typed in many carbon copies. Today printed: *Sbornicul*, Ed. Renașterea, Cluj, Romania, 2015.

*** 1970: *Saint Herman of Alaska*, The Orthodox Church of America. Printed with the blessing of His Eminence, The Most Reverend Kiprian, Archbishop of Philadelphia and Pennsylvania for the canonization of St. Herman of Alaska, Wilkes-Barre, Pennsylvania.

*** 1976: *Viața și faptele Sfântului Ierarh Calinic de la Cernica, Episcopul Râmnicului*, [Life and Facts of Saint Callinicus of Chernika, Bishop of Ramnic], București, Romania. See also https://oca.org/saints/lives/2012/04/11/101059-st-callinicus-of-cernica-the-bishop-of-rimnicului-in-romania.

*** 1979: *Petite Philocalie de la prière du coeur*, traduite et présentée par Jean Gouillard, Éditions du Seuil, Paris, France.

*** 1980: *Little Russian Philokalia, vol. I, St. Seraphim of Sarov*, St. Herman of Alaska Brotherhood,

Platina, California. See also an excellent text with pictures on internet at http://www.symeon-anthony.info/StSeraphimSarov/ StSeraphimSarov.htm

*** 1981: *The Philokalia: The Complete Text*, Compyled by St. Nikodimos of the Holy Mountain and St. Makarios of Corinth, volume 2. Transl. by G.E.H. Palmer, Philip Sherrard and Kallistos Ware, Faber and Faber Inc., London, UK.

*** 1982: *The Philokalia: The Complete Text*, Compyled by St. Nikodimos of the Holy Mountain and St. Makarios of Corinth, volume 1. Transl. by G.E.H. Palmer, Philip Sherrard and Kallistos Ware, Faber and Faber Inc., London, UK.

*** 1986: *The Philokalia: The Complete Text*, Compyled by St. Nikodimos of the Holy Mountain and St. Makarios of Corinth, volume 3. Transl. by G.E.H. Palmer, Philip Sherrard and Kallistos Ware, Faber and Faber Inc., London, UK.

*** 1989: *Little Russian Philokalia, vol. III, St. Herman*, New Valaam Monastery, Alaska. St. Herman Press.

*** 1992: *The Tradition of St. Paisius Velichkovsky in Romania and America Today*, In *The Orthodox Word*, St. Herman of Alaska Brotherhood, Platina, California, No. 178: 5-50.

*** 1994a: *Little Russian Philokalia, vol. IV, Saint Paisius Velichkovsky*, transl. Fr. Seraphim Rose. New Valaam Monastery, Alaska, St. Herman Press/St.Paisius Abbey Press.

*** 1994b: *The bicentennial of St. Paisius*

Velichkovsky. *[New] Akathist to Our Holy and God-Bearing Father Paisius Velichkovsky. Miracles of St. Paisius Velichkovsky and Other Incidents from His God-pleasing Life from "The Chronology of the Holy Monastery of Neamts" by Andronicus the Elder* (Excerpted from *Contribuția românească la personalitatea, opera și amintirea Starețului Paisie Velicikovski*, by Archimandrite Ciprian Zaharia, Abbot of the Holy Monastery of Bistritsa-Neamts, 1985). *A Letter from St. Paisius's Elder*. In *The Orthodox Word*, St. Herman of Alaska Brotherhood, Platina, California, No. 178: 257, 265, 267-280, 288.

*** 1996a: *Învățăturile lui Neagoe Basarab către fiul său Theodosie* [The Teachings of Neagoe Basarab to His Son Theodosius], translated from slavonic and edited by G. Mihăilă. Ed. Roza Vânturilor, București, Romania.

*** 1996b: *Praying with the Orthodox Tradition*, with a Foreword by Kallistos Ware. St. Vladimir's Seminary Press, Crestwood, New York.

*** 1999: *Patericul* [Patericon, Egyptian Patericon or Apophthegmata Patrum], Editura Reîntregirea, Alba Iulia, Romania. See also *The Sayings of the Desert Fathers*, which is a part of the Egyptian Patericon, transl. Sister Benedicta Ward, The Sisters of the Love of God, Cistercian Publications, Kalamazoo, Michigan, 1975.

*** 2000: *Brother Michael "the Silent" of Valaam*, in the Series *Complete Valaam Patericon*. In *The Orthodox Word*, St. Herman of Alaska Brotherhood, Platina, California, No. 210: 29-33.

*** 2001: *Father Arseny, 1893-1973, Priest, Prisoner, Spiritual Father.* Compiled by the servant of God Alexander, transl. Vera Bouteneff. St. Vladimir's Seminary Press, *SVP*, Crestwood, New York.

*** 2002: *Cuviosul Paisie de la Neamț. Autobiografia și Viețile unui stareț, urmate de Așezăminte și alte texte* [Blessed Paisius of Neamts. Autobiography and Life Stories of a Starets, Followed by Rules of Monastic Life and Other Texts]. With excerpts from Elia Citterio's introductory study, *Paisij Velickovskij, Autobiografia di uno starets* (Editioni Scitti Monastici, Abbazia di Praglia, 1988). Edited by Deacon Ioan I. Ică jr. Editura Deisis, Sibiu, Romania.

*** 2011: *Some sayings of Saint Seraphim of Sarov*, https://www.orthocuban.com/2011/08/some-sayings-of-saint-seraphim-of-sarov/

*** 2012: *Viața și Acatistul Sfântului Cuvios Paisie de la Neamț* (Life and Akathist of Saint Paisius of Neamts], Institutul Biblic și de Misiune Ortodoxă (IBMBOR), București, Romania.

*** 2018: *The Venerable Fathers of Optina Hermitage, Spiritual Disciples of St. Paisius (Velichkovsky).* From the Synaxarion by Hieromonk Makarios of Simonos Petra. On website of the Holy Monastery of Saint Paisius, Safford, Arizona. https://stpaisiusmonastery.org/about-the-monastery/life-of-st-paisius/optina-elders/

Bălan, Ioanichie, 1996: *Romanian Paterikon*, vol.1, St. Herman of Alaska Brotherhood, Platina, California.

Bălan, Ioanichie, Archimandrite, 2001: *Elder*

Cleopa of Sihastria: In the Tradition of St. Paisius Velichkovsky. Translated with additions by Mother Cassiana. New Varatec Publishing, Lake George, Colorado.

Belonick, Stephen, The Very Rev., 1998: *A Journey through Great Lent*, Ligh and Life Publishing, Minneapolis, Minnesota.

Bloom, Anthony, Metropolitan, 1966: *Living Prayer*. Templegate Publishers, Springfield, Illinois.

Bloom, Anthony, Archbishop, 1970: *School for Prayer*. A Libra Book, London, UK.

Bloom, Anthony, Metropolitan of Sourozh, 1989: *Practical Prayer, An Interview with Metropolitan Anthony of Sourozh*. Conciliar Press, Ben Lomond, California.

Braga, Roman, Archimandrite, 1996: *Exploring the Inner Universe. Joy – the Mystery of Life*. HDM Press, Monastery of the Dormition of the Mother of God, Rives Junction, Michigan.

Braga, Roman, Archimandrite, 1997: *On the Way of Faith. Faith, Freedom and Love*. HDM Press, Monastery of the Dormition of the Mother of God, Rives Junction, Michigan.

Brumfield, William, 2014: *Optina Pustyn: Spiritual Retreat of Tolstoy and Dostoyevsky*, in „Rossiyskaya gazeta" (www.pravoslavie.ru/74360.html).

Calciu, George Fr., 1997: *Christ is calling you, a course in catacomb pastorship*. St. Herman of Alaska Brotherhood, Platina, California.

Christensen, Damascene, Hieromonk, 2003: *Father Seraphim Rose, His Life and Works*. St. Herman of Alaska Brotherhood, Platina, California.

Christensen, Damascene, Hieromonk, 2008: *Saved from Fire*. In *The Orthodox Word*, St. Herman of Alaska Brotherhood, Platina, California, No. 260: 105-109.

Clément, Olivier, 1977: *La prière de Jesus*, in Jacques Serr et Olivier Clement, *Spiritualité orientale*, no.6 bis, Abbaye de Bellefontaine, Begrolles-en-Mauges (Maine-et-Loire), France.

Cleopa Ilie, Arhimandrit, 2012: *Predici la praznice împărătești și la sfinți de peste an*, [Homilies on Great Feasts and on Saints during the Liturgical Year], Editura Episcopiei Romanului, România.

Colliander, Tito, 1985: *Way of the Ascetics*, St. Vladimir Seminary Press, Crestwood, New York.

Coniaris, Anthony M., 1998: *Philokalia, The Bible of Orthodox Spirituality*, Light and Life Publishing Company, Minneapolis.

Crainic, Nichifor, 1993: *Sfințenia, împlinirea umanului* [Holiness is the completion of human essence], Ed. Trinitas, Iași, Romania.

Cristian, Roxana, 2016: *Icoana Rugului aprins de la Mănăstirea Antim* [The Icon of Burning Bush from the Antim Monastery], in *Însemnări la apusul soarelui*, Ed. Rosmarin, București, Romania.

Daniil, Monahul (Sandu Tudor), 1997: Acatiste. Imn-Acatist la Rugul Aprins al Maicii Domnului,

Acatistul Sfantului Ioan Bogoslovul, Acatistul Sfântului Calinic Cernicanul [Acathysts. Acathyst-Hymn at Burning Bush of Theotokos, Acathyst to Saint John the Bogoslov, Acathyst to Saint Calinic of Cernica]. Ed. Anastasia, Bucureşti, Romania.

Desartovici, L.S., Anamaria Rus, Cosmina Tamas, 2000: *60 de istorisiri minunate adunate de la Sfinţii Părinţi* [Sixty wonderful stories gathered from the Holy Fathers]. Asociaţia Română pentru Cultură şi Ortodoxie, Bucureşti, Romania.

Diaconu, Gheorghe, 2017: The Image of Saint Paisius Velichkovsky and the Exhumation [of] His Relics (II), Revista Teologica, 99, nr. 2: 228-261.

Dumitru, Antonel, 2011: *Sfântul Ierarh Calinic de la Mănăstirea Cernica – 150 ani de la înveşnicirea sa* [Saint Hierarch Callinicus of the Chernika Monastery – 150 years from his entrance into eternity]. In *Lumina*, 11 aprilie 2018.

Drozdek, Adam, 2014: Monastic Worldview of Paisii Velichkovskii. PERSPEC†IVA, Legnickie Studia Teologiczno-Historyczne, Poland, Rok XIII, 2014, nr 2 (25):7–23.

Every, George, Richard Harries, Kallistos Ware, 1984: *The Time of the Spirit. Readings through the Christian Year*. St. Vladimir's Seminary Press, Crestwood, New York.

Evdokimov, Paul, 1985: *The Sacrament of Love*, St. Vladimir's Seminary Press, Crestwood, New York.

Gerasim Eliel, R. Monk, 1989: *Father Gerasim of New Valaam*, in *The Acquisition of the Holy Spirit in*

Rusia Series, vol. 5, New Valaam Monastery, Alaska, St. Herman Press.

Groza, Horia Ion, 2006: *Treptele de văzduh ale sufletului și setea de Dumnezeu* [The Ladder of the Inner Sky and the Thirst for God], Criterion Publishing, București, Romania.

Groza, Horia Ion, 2011: Mișcarea spirituală Rugul Aprins de la Mănăstirea Antim [The Spiritual Movement "The Burning Bush" from Antim Monastery]. In *Origini/Romanian Roots*, LiterArt XXI, Bucuresti, Romania/ Atlanta, Georgia. Vol.XV, Part II, July-December:68-74

Groza, Horia Ion, 2016: *Discovering the Sacred Time of Our Life*. Reflection Publishing, Sacramento, California.

Groza, Horia Ion, 2018: *Living the Sacred Time of Our Life*. Reflection Publishing, Sacramento, California.

Joantă, Seraphim, Bishop, 1992: *Romania. Its Hesychast Tradition and Culture*. St. Xenia Skete, Wildwood, California.

Kallistos, Bishop of Diokleia, 1986: *The Power of the Name, The Jesus Prayer in Orthodox Spirituality*, SLG Press, Oxford, England.

Kallistos, Ware, Bishop, 1996: *Foreword to "Praying with the Orthodox Tradition"*, compiled by Stefano Parenti, transl. Paula Clifford. Saint Vladimir's Seminary Press, *SVS Press,* Crestwood, New York.

Laurus, Metropolitan, 2004: *A Homily on St. Paisius Velichkovsky. In Commemoration on the 210th Anniversary of his Repose.* Russian Orthodox Church Outside of Russia. St. Paisius Monastery, Safford, Arizona. http://stpaisiusmonastery.org/

Metrophanes, Schema-monk, 1976: *Blessed Paisius Velichkovsky - The Life and Ascetic Labors of Our Father, Elder Paisius, Archimandrite of The Holy Moldavian Monasteries Niamets and Sekoul.* Optina Version. Saint Herman of Alaska Brotherhood, Platina, California.

Metrophanes, Schema-monk, 1994: *Blessed Paisius Velichkovsky - The Man Behind the Philokalia.* Includes *Chapter VII, The Philokalia* and *Chapter VIII, The Legacy of Blessed Paisius* (see pages 251-253 for the quote from *Pravoslavny Blagovestnik*, No.3/1967 in San Francisco). Saint Paisius Abbey. Saint Herman of Alaska Brotherhood, Platina, California. First Printing in 1976.

Nun Nina, of St. Paisius' Holy Cross Skete, 1995: *The Spiritual Face of Romania Today.* In *The Orthodox Word*, St. Herman of Alaska Brotherhood, Platina, California, No.184: 205-207.

Oleska, Michael, V.Rev., 2018: *Everyday Wonders. Stories of God's providence.* Ancient Faith Publishing, Chesterton, Indiana.

Polkinghorne, John, Nicholas Beale, 2009: *Questions of Truth. Fifty-one responsese to Questions about God, Science, and Belief.* Westminster John Knox Press, Louisville, Kentucky.

Princess Ileana of Romania, H.R.H, 1959: *Introduction to the Jesus Prayer*, Light and Life, Minneapolis, Minnesota.

Scrima, André, 2000: *Timpul rugului aprins* [The Time of the Burning Bush]. Humanitas, București, Romania.

Scrima, André, 2008: *Ortodoxia și încercarea comunismului* [The Orthodoxy and the Attempt of the Communism]. Humanitas, București, Romania.

St. John Climacus, 1982: *The Ladder of Divine Ascent*. Paulist Press, Mahwah, New Jersey.

Stakhovich, Maria, 1995: *Elder Michael, the last great mystic of Valaam*, in *The Orthodox Word*, St. Herman of Alaska Brotherhood, Platina, California, No. 185: 259-265.

Staniloae, Dumitru, 1979: *Despre istoria isihasmului în ortodoxia română*, [About the History of Hesychasm in the Romanian Orthodoxy], in *Filocalia*, vol. VIII, Editura Institutului Biblic, București, Romania.

Staniloae, Dumitru, 1980: *Theology and the Church*, transl. Robert Barringer. Saint Vladimir's Seminary Press, SVS Press, Crestwood, New York.

Staniloae, Dumitru, 1996: *Prayer and Holiness*, transl. by The Sisters of the Love of God 1982, SLG Press, Convent of the Incarnation, Fairacres, Oxford, England.

Staniloae, Dumitru, 1998: *Revelation and Knowledge of the Triune God*, volume 1 from *The*

Experience of God, Orthodox Dogmatic Theology. Holy Cross Orthodox Press, Brookline, Massachusetts.

Staniloae, Dumitru, Priest Professor, 2002: *Orthodox Spirituality. A Practical Guide for the Faithful and a Definitive Manual for the Scholar*, transl. Archim. Jerome Newville and Otilia Kloos. St. Tikhon's Seminary Press, Pennsylvania.

Telea, Marius, 1995: *Mișcarea isihastică și legăturile ei cu românii* [The Hesychastic Movement and its Relation with Romanians] in *Revista Teologică*, Sibiu, Romania, nr. 1: 81-91.

Un moine de l'Église d'Orient, 1963: *La prière de Jesus*. Éditions de Chevetogne. Chevetogne, Belgium.

Ware, Timothy, (Bishop Kallistos of Diokleia), 1987: *The Orthodox Church*, Penguin Books Ltd., London, and Viking Penguin Inc., New York.

Waterfield, Robin, 1987: *René Guénon and the future of the West, The life and writings of a 20th-century metaphysician*, Crucible, Great Britain.

Zaharia, Ciprian, Archimandrite, Abbot of the Holy Monastery of Bistritsa-Neamts, 1985: Contribuția românească la personalitatea, opera și amintirea Starețului Paisie Velicikovski (1722-1794) [The Romanian Contribution to the personality, work and remembrance of the Abbot Paisius Velichkovsky]. Excerpts can be found under *Miracles of St. Paisius Velichkovsky… from "The Chronology of the Holy Monastery of Neamts" by Andronicus the Elder* in *The Orthodox Word, The bicentennial of St. Paisius Velichkovsky*, St. Herman of Alaska Brotherhood,

Platina, California, 1994, No. 178: 267-280.

Zamfirescu, Dan, 1996: *Paisianismul, un moment românesc în istoria spiritualității europene*, [The Paisianism, a Romanian Moment in the European Spiritual History]. Ed. Roza Vânturilor, București, Romania.

Bibles quoted

The Orthodox Study Bible (SAAS™ and NKJV®), St. Athanasius Academy of Orthodox Theology, Elk Grove, California, 2008.

Books published by Horia Ion Groza

HORIA ION GROZA

DISCOVERING THE SACRED TIME OF OUR LIFE

Reflection Publishing
(August 29, 2016)
Language: English
ISBN-13: 978-1936629466
Paperback: 338 pages
Product Dimensions: 5.8 x 0.7 x 8.3 inches
Price: $16.98
Available at Amazon, Barnes and Noble

HORIA ION GROZA

LIVING THE SACRED TIME OF OUR LIFE

Reflection Publishing
(February 25, 2018)
Language: English
ISBN-13: 978-1936629510
Paperback: 452 pages
Product Dimensions: 5.8 x 0.9 x 8.3 inches
Price: $18.85
Available at Amazon, Barnes and Noble

VIAȚA MAICII DOMNULUI

AȘA CUM ESTE CUNOSCUTĂ ÎN TRADIȚIA BISERICII ORTODOXE

Reflection Publishing

Reflection Publishing
(June 1, 2011)
Language: Romanian
ISBN-13: 978-0979761843
Paperback: 100 pages
Product Dimensions: 6 x 0.2 x 9 inches
Price: $11.95
Available at Amazon, Barnes and Noble

Reflection Publishing, P.O. Box 2182
Citrus Heights, California 95611-2182
E-mail: info@reflectionbooks.com
www.reflectionbooks.com

CPSIA information can be obtained
at www.ICGtesting.com
Printed in the USA
FSHW020004271221
87190FS

9 781936 629527